THE
FIRST
CHRISTMAS

THE
FIRST
CHRISTMAS

What the Gospels Really Teach About Jesus's Birth

MARCUS BORG &
JOHN DOMINIC CROSSAN

HarperOne
A Division of HarperCollinsPublishers

HarperOne

THE FIRST CHRISTMAS: *What the Gospels Really Teach About Jesus's Birth*.
Copyright © 2007 by Marcus J. Borg and John Dominic Crossan. All rights reserved.
Printed in the United States of America. No part of this book may be used or repro-
duced in any manner whatsoever without written permission except in the case of
brief quotations embodied in critical articles and reviews. For information address
HarperCollins Publishers, 10 East 53rd Street, New York, NY 10022.

HarperCollins books may be purchased for educational, business, or sales promo-
tional use. For information please write: Special Markets Department, HarperCollins
Publishers, 10 East 53rd Street, New York, NY 10022.

HarperCollins Web site: http://www.harpercollins.com

HarperCollins®, 📖®, and HarperOne™ are trademarks of HarperCollins
Publishers, Inc.

FIRST EDITION

Library of Congress Cataloging-in-Publication Data is available.
ISBN-10: 0-06-143070-6
ISBN-13: 978-0-06-143070-1

07 08 09 10 11   RRD(H)   10 9 8 7 6 5 4 3 2 1

CONTENTS

Preface *vii*

PART I PARABLE, OVERTURE, AND CONTEXT

  1 The Stories of the First Christmas 3

  2 Parables as Overtures 25

  3 The Context of the Christmas Stories 55

PART II GENEALOGY, CONCEPTION, AND BIRTH

  4 Genealogy as Destiny 81

  5 An Angel Comes to Mary 99

  6 In David's City of Bethlehem 129

PART III LIGHT, FULFILLMENT, AND JOY

  7 Light Against the Darkness 171

  8 Jesus as the Fulfillment of Prophecy 199

  9 Joy to the World 227

Appendix 1 *The Genealogies of Jesus in Matthew and Luke* *245*

Appendix 2 *Luke's Parallelism Between Jesus and John the Baptizer* *251*

Appendix 3 *Jesus's Coming-of-Age in Luke* *253*

  Acknowledgments *257*

  Notes *259*

PREFACE

This book, *The First Christmas,* treats what may be the best-known stories in the world. The stories of Jesus's birth are the foundation of the world's most widely observed holiday. Christmas is celebrated by the world's two billion Christians, a number about twice that of the next largest religion, Islam. Moreover, because of the cultural and commercial importance of Christmas in Western culture and beyond, it is observed by many non-Christians as well. Indeed, no other religious holiday is so widely commemorated by people who are outside of the tradition that originated it.

The idea to write this book about the stories of the first Christmas flowed out of our previous collaboration, *The Last Week.* There we treated the last week of Jesus's life as told by Mark, the earliest gospel. From Jesus's entry into Jerusalem to his execution and resurrection, Mark provides a day-by-day account of Jesus's final week. Known by Christians as Holy Week, it is the most sacred week of the Christian year.

For more than one reason, this book is an obvious sequel. *The Last Week* is about the end of the life of Jesus; *The First Christmas* is about the beginning. Together, the stories of his birth and the stories of his last week are like bookends that frame the gospel stories of his public activity, his mission and message. The stories of his birth, as we will suggest, are like overtures to the story of Jesus, just as Holy Week is its finale.

A second reason: just as Holy Week is the most sacred time of the Christian year, Christmas is the second most sacred time. Indeed, in contemporary Western culture and even for many Christians, the commemoration of Christmas exceeds the commemoration of Easter.

Because of the importance of Christmas, how we understand the stories of Jesus's birth matters. What we think they're about—how we hear them, read them, interpret them—matters.

They are often sentimentalized. And, of course, there is emotional power in them. They touch the deepest of human yearnings: for light in the darkness, for the fulfillment of our hopes, for a different kind of world. Moreover, for many Christians, they are associated with their earliest memories of childhood. Christmas has emotional power.

But the stories of Jesus's birth are more than sentimental. The stories of the first Christmas are both personal and political. They speak of personal and political transformation. Set in their first-century context, they are comprehensive and passionate visions of another way of seeing life and of living our lives.

They challenge the common life, the status quo, of most times and places. Even as they are tidings of comfort and joy, they are edgy and challenging. They confront "normalcy," what we call "the normalcy of civilization"—the way most societies, most human cultures, have been and are organized.

When we conceived this book, we thought we would call it *The First Week*. Doing so would echo the title of *The Last Week* and signal that these books are companion volumes, "bookends." But our editor wisely suggested that *The First Christmas* would be a better title. The echo of *The Last Week* might be missed. Moreover, the birth stories are not about Jesus's first week in the same way that Mark gives us a day-by-day account of Jesus's final week. Instead, we have two chapters at the beginning of two gospels, Matthew and Luke. In each, the two chapters introduce the story of Jesus. They are, as we will suggest, parabolic overtures to the story of Jesus. And they cover more than his first week. They report his genealogy and conception, his birth and infancy, and one concludes with a story of him at age twelve.

So this book is about the "first Christmas" in the sense that it treats the stories of the first Christmas, the nativity stories of Jesus. They are richer and more challenging than is commonly imagined.

We are not concerned with the factuality of the birth stories. Though we comment on this issue and controversy in Chapter 2, our concern is neither to defend them as factual nor to trash them as nonfactual. Rather, we focus on their meanings. What *did* and *do* these stories *mean*?

Our task is twofold. The first is historical: to exposit these stories and their meanings in their first-century context. The second is contemporary: to treat their meanings for Christian understanding and commitment today.

Both tasks are historical and theological. The first-century context is not simply historical, but also theological. It concerns the conflict between an imperial theology and a theology grounded in the God of Israel as known in the Bible and Jesus. Our twenty-first-century context is also historical and theological. What do the stories of Jesus's birth mean in our contemporary historical context?

We think hearing their ancient and contemporary meanings matters particularly for American Christians today. To say the obvious, America is in the powerful and perilous position of being the empire of our day. As we will see, the stories of the first Christmas are pervasively anti-imperial. In our setting, what does it mean to affirm with the Christmas stories that Jesus is the Son of God (and the emperor is not), that Jesus is the savior of the world (and the emperor is not), that Jesus is Lord (and the emperor is not), that Jesus is the way to peace on earth (and the emperor is not). The repetition risks growing tiresome.

There is a political meaning and challenge in these stories, both in their ancient setting and today. Of course, these stories are not "only" political—they are also deeply personal. They speak, and speak powerfully, about our deepest yearnings and about God's promises and passion. They are religious in the way the Bible as a whole is religious: life with the God of Israel, the God of Jesus, is both personal and political. The personal and political meanings can be distinguished but not separated without betraying one or the other. And because the political meaning of these stories has commonly been overlooked, we highlight it in much of this book.

Doing so involves no denial of the way these stories also speak to our lives as individuals. They are about light in our darkness, the fulfillment of our deepest yearnings, and the birth of Christ within us. They are about us—our hopes and fears. And they are about a different kind of world. God's dream for us is not simply peace of mind, but peace on earth.

PART I

PARABLE, OVERTURE, AND CONTEXT

CHAPTER ONE

————— ◆◆◆ —————

THE STORIES OF THE
FIRST CHRISTMAS

In this chapter, we introduce the stories of the first Christmas. Note the plural: we do not have *a* story of the first
Christmas, but two. They are found in Matthew and
Luke, two of the four gospels of the New Testament. Each
begins with two chapters about the birth of Jesus.

We begin with the texts of Matthew 1–2 and Luke 1–2. We
do so for more than one reason. Though general features of
the stories are well known, the more specific details are not.
Moreover, people seldom encounter them as "whole narratives"; most often they hear and know them in parts.

A third reason: Matthew's and Luke's stories are quite
different from each other. Many Christians as well as non-
Christians are not familiar with how different they are. Seeing
these differences is utterly crucial to understanding why we

(and contemporary biblical scholars generally) see them as we do. It is the foundation for what follows in this book. And so we present the stories by imagining a Christmas pageant based on each.

Matthew's Pageant

Matthew's birth story is significantly shorter than Luke's. His gospel starts with a genealogy of Jesus, which takes up about two-thirds of his first chapter. Without the genealogy, the whole of Matthew's birth story takes only 31 verses. Luke's story, with 132, is about four times as long.

Suppose we imagine a Christmas pageant based on Matthew alone. What would it be like? It would begin with a whole lot of begetting, presumably read by a narrator. Matthew mentions forty-two generations of Jesus's genealogy, although only forty are actually reported. We do not print Matthew's genealogy here, but in Appendix 1. Then, in the last part of his chapter 1, his narrative of the events surrounding the birth of Jesus commences.

Scene One: Conception of Jesus and Joseph's Dilemma

The first scene that could be dramatized in our imaginary pageant occurs at the end of Matthew 1:

> Now the birth of Jesus the Messiah took place in this way. When his mother Mary had been engaged to Joseph, but before they lived together, she was found to be with child from the Holy Spirit. Her husband Joseph, being a righteous man and unwilling to expose her to public disgrace, planned to dismiss her quietly. But just when he had re-

solved to do this, an angel of the Lord appeared to him in a dream and said, "Joseph, son of David, do not be afraid to take Mary as your wife, for the child conceived in her is from the Holy Spirit. She will bear a son, and you are to name him Jesus, for he will save his people from their sins." All this took place to fulfill what had been spoken by the Lord through the prophet:

> *"Look, the virgin shall conceive and bear a son,*
>   *and they shall name him Emmanuel,"*

which means, "God is with us." When Joseph awoke from sleep, he did as the angel of the Lord commanded him; he took her as his wife, but had no marital relations with her until she had borne a son; and he named him Jesus. (1:18–25)

In this first scene, Joseph is the main character. Mary neither speaks nor receives any revelation (and does not throughout Matthew's story as a whole). Jesus's birth is mentioned only in a passing phrase in the last verse of the chapter. Even here, Joseph is the subject of the sentence: "He had no marital relations with her [Mary] *until she had borne a son;* and he named him Jesus" (1:25). There is no story of the birth itself, no swaddling clothes, no stable, no manger, no angels singing to shepherds on the night of Jesus's birth. All of these are from Luke.

Our dramatization moves to the second chapter of Matthew. In this chapter, the main character is King Herod, known to history as Herod the Great, with a major supporting role played by the wise men. Of course, Mary, Joseph, and Jesus are also in this chapter—but what they do is in response to Herod's actions. Herod drives the plot, which unfolds in five scenes.

Scene Two: Star, Wise Men, and Herod

King Herod's court in Jerusalem is the setting:

> In the time of King Herod, after Jesus was born in Beth-
> lehem of Judea, wise men from the East came to Jeru-
> salem, asking, "Where is the child who has been born
> King of the Jews? For we observed his star at its rising,
> and have come to pay him homage." When King Herod
> heard this, he was frightened, and all Jerusalem with
> him; and calling together all the chief priests and scribes
> of the people, he inquired of them where the Messiah
> was to be born. They told him, "In Bethlehem of Judea;
> for so it has been written by the prophet:
>
> > *'And you, Bethlehem, in the land of Judah,*
> >   *are by no means least among the rulers of Judah;*
> > *for from you shall come a ruler*
> >   *who is to shepherd my people Israel.'"*
>
> Then Herod secretly called for the wise men and
> learned from them the exact time when the star had ap-
> peared. Then he sent them to Bethlehem, saying, "Go
> and search diligently for the child; and when you have
> found him, bring me word so that I may also go and pay
> him homage." (2:1–8)

We begin to see Herod's plot. Alarmed at the prospect of
a rival king, Herod tells the wise men to bring him word of
the child's whereabouts, so that he can also pay him homage.
Of course, that is not what he has in mind; he plans to kill the
child.

Scene Three: Adoration of the Magi

The wise men—the Magi—follow the star to "the house" (not a stable), where they find Mary and Jesus. What has been known for centuries as the "Adoration of the Magi" then occurs:

> When they had heard the king, they set out; and there, ahead of them, went the star that they had seen at its rising, until it stopped over the place where the child was. When they saw that the star had stopped, they were overwhelmed with joy. On entering the house, they saw the child with Mary his mother; and they knelt down and paid him homage. Then, opening their treasure chests, they offered him gifts of gold, frankincense, and myrrh. And having been warned in a dream not to return to Herod, they left for their own country by another road. (2:9–12)

At the end of the scene, the wise men are told in a dream not to return to Herod to tell him where the child is. They follow the instructions in the dream and return home by a different route.

Scene Four: Flight into Egypt to Escape Herod's Plot

Though Joseph is the main character in this scene, Herod's murderous intent continues to drive the plot:

> Now after they had left, an angel of the Lord appeared to Joseph in a dream and said, "Get up, take the child and his mother, and flee to Egypt, and remain there until I tell you; for Herod is about to search for the child, to

destroy him." Then Joseph got up, took the child and his
mother by night, and went to Egypt, and remained there
until the death of Herod. This was to fulfill what had
been spoken by the Lord through the prophet, "Out of
Egypt I have called my son." (2:13–15)

The family lives in Egypt until the death of Herod.

Scene Five: Herod's Slaughter of the Infants

We are back in Herod's court. Realizing that the wise men are
not coming back, he orders the killing of children in and around
Bethlehem who were two years old or under. The slaughter is
followed by much "wailing and loud lamentation":

When Herod saw that he had been tricked by the wise
men, he was infuriated, and he sent and killed all the
children in and around Bethlehem who were two years
old or under, according to the time that he had learned
from the wise men. Then was fulfilled what had been
spoken through the prophet Jeremiah:

"A voice was heard in Ramah,
　wailing and loud lamentation,
Rachel weeping for her children;
　she refused to be consoled, because they are no more."
(2:16–18)

Scene Six: Return from Egypt and Move to Nazareth

Herod's death triggers this scene. We are back in Egypt, where
Joseph again has a dream in which an angel comes to him:

When Herod died, an angel of the Lord suddenly appeared in a dream to Joseph in Egypt and said, "Get up, take the child and his mother, and go to the land of Israel, for those who were seeking the child's life are dead." Then Joseph got up, took the child and his mother, and went to the land of Israel. But when he heard that Archelaus was ruling over Judea in place of his father Herod, he was afraid to go there. And after being warned in a dream, he went away to the district of Galilee. There he made his home in a town called Nazareth, so that what had been spoken through the prophets might be fulfilled, "He will be called a Nazorean." (2:19–23)

Note that Joseph intends to bring his family back to Bethlehem, their home in Matthew. But because of the deadly reputation of the new king, Herod's son Archelaus, the family moves to Galilee instead, to the village of Nazareth.

This is the last scene in Matthew's story of Jesus's birth and the final scene in our imaginary pageant based on Matthew. From here, Matthew jumps forward in time thirty years. At the beginning of chapter 3, John the Baptizer is preaching in the wilderness and Jesus is a mature adult who goes to be with him. There is no mention of Jesus's youth, except that he grew up in Nazareth.

Indeed, it is surprising how little of Matthew's birth story is about Jesus; Jesus is almost "off stage." Of course, in one sense, *all* of it is about Jesus—but so many familiar elements are missing. There is no story of a journey to Bethlehem, no story of his birth, no story of angels singing in the night sky, no story of shepherds coming to adore him. In addition, there is no story of his circumcision, no story of him being blessed in the temple as an infant by Simeon and Anna, no story of him later at age twelve in the temple amazing the teachers with his wisdom. All of these are in Luke. Instead, the narrative dynamic of Matthew's story focuses on Joseph and his dilemma and on Herod and his unsuccessful attempt to destroy Jesus.

LUKE'S PAGEANT

We turn now to imagining a Christmas pageant based on the first two chapters of Luke. Unlike Matthew's birth story, Luke's does not include a genealogy. Instead, Luke attaches a genealogy to the story of the baptism of Jesus at the end of Luke 3. And as we did with Matthew's, we print it in Appendix 1. The two genealogies, as we will see in Chapter 4, are quite different from each other.

Because of the length of Luke's story (recall that it is four times as long as Matthew's), it would be tedious to do this scene by scene as we did with Matthew. Instead, we print Luke's story with concise section headings and then comment about the features that a pageant based on Luke would have. After a four-verse dedication of his gospel, Luke's story of the events of the first Christmas begins in 1:5.

Conception of John the Baptizer

In the days of King Herod of Judea, there was a priest named Zechariah, who belonged to the priestly order of Abijah. His wife was a descendant of Aaron, and her name was Elizabeth. Both of them were righteous before God, living blamelessly according to all the commandments and regulations of the Lord. But they had no children, because Elizabeth was barren, and both were getting on in years.

Once when he was serving as priest before God and his section was on duty, he was chosen by lot, according to the custom of the priesthood, to enter the sanctuary of the Lord and offer incense. Now at the time of the incense offering, the whole assembly of the people was praying outside. Then there appeared to him an angel of the Lord, standing at the right side of the altar of incense. When Zechariah saw him, he was terrified; and fear overwhelmed him. But the angel said to him, "Do not be afraid, Zechariah, for your prayer has been heard. Your wife Elizabeth will bear you a son, and you will name him John. You will have joy and gladness, and many will rejoice at his birth, for he will be great in the sight of the Lord. He must never drink wine or strong drink; even before his birth he will be filled with the Holy Spirit. He will turn many of the people of Israel to the Lord their God. With the spirit and power of Elijah he will go before him, to turn the hearts of parents to their children, and the disobedient to the wisdom of the righteous, to make ready a people prepared for the Lord." Zechariah said to the angel, "How will I know that this is so? For I am an old man, and my wife is getting on in years." The angel replied, "I am Gabriel. I stand in the presence of God, and I have been sent to speak to you and to bring you this good news. But now, because you did not believe my words, which will be fulfilled in their time, you will become mute, unable to speak, until the day these things occur."

Meanwhile the people were waiting for Zechariah, and wondered at his delay in the sanctuary. When he did

come out, he could not speak to them, and they realized
that he had seen a vision in the sanctuary. He kept motioning to them and remained unable to speak. When his
time of service was ended, he went to his home.

After those days his wife Elizabeth conceived, and for
five months she remained in seclusion. She said, "This is
what the Lord has done for me when he looked favorably on me and took away the disgrace I have endured
among my people." (1:5–25)

Conception of Jesus (the Annunciation)

In the sixth month the angel Gabriel was sent by God to
a town in Galilee called Nazareth, to a virgin engaged to
a man whose name was Joseph, of the house of David.
The virgin's name was Mary. And he came to her and
said, "Greetings, favored one! The Lord is with you."
But she was much perplexed by his words and pondered
what sort of greeting this might be. The angel said to
her, "Do not be afraid, Mary, for you have found favor
with God. And now, you will conceive in your womb
and bear a son, and you will name him Jesus. He will be
great, and will be called the Son of the Most High, and
the Lord God will give to him the throne of his ancestor
David. He will reign over the house of Jacob forever, and
of his kingdom there will be no end." Mary said to the
angel, "How can this be, since I am a virgin?" The angel
said to her, "The Holy Spirit will come upon you, and
the power of the Most High will overshadow you; therefore the child to be born will be holy; he will be called
Son of God. And now, your relative Elizabeth in her old

age has also conceived a son; and this is the sixth month for her who was said to be barren. For nothing will be impossible with God." Then Mary said, "Here am I, the servant of the Lord; let it be with me according to your word." Then the angel departed from her. (1:26–38)

Mary's Visit to Elizabeth and Hymn (the Magnificat)

In those days Mary set out and went with haste to a Judean town in the hill country, where she entered the house of Zechariah and greeted Elizabeth. When Elizabeth heard Mary's greeting, the child leaped in her womb. And Elizabeth was filled with the Holy Spirit and exclaimed with a loud cry, "Blessed are you among women, and blessed is the fruit of your womb. And why has this happened to me, that the mother of my Lord comes to me? For as soon as I heard the sound of your greeting, the child in my womb leaped for joy. And blessed is she who believed that there would be a fulfillment of what was spoken to her by the Lord."

And Mary said,

> *"My soul magnifies the Lord,*
> *and my spirit rejoices in God my Savior,*
> *for he has looked with favor on the lowliness of his servant.*
> *Surely, from now on all generations will call me*
> *blessed;*
> *for the Mighty One has done great things for me,*
> *and holy is his name.*
> *His mercy is for those who fear him*
> *from generation to generation.*

He has shown strength with his arm;
*   he has scattered the proud in the thoughts of their*
*   hearts.*
He has brought down the powerful from their thrones,
*   and lifted up the lowly;*
he has filled the hungry with good things,
*   and sent the rich away empty.*
He has helped his servant Israel,
*   in remembrance of his mercy,*
according to the promise he made to our ancestors,
*   to Abraham and to his descendants forever."*

And Mary remained with her about three months and then returned to her home. (1:39–56)

Birth of John the Baptizer and Hymn (the Benedictus)

Now the time came for Elizabeth to give birth, and she bore a son. Her neighbors and relatives heard that the Lord had shown his great mercy to her, and they rejoiced with her.

On the eighth day they came to circumcise the child, and they were going to name him Zechariah after his father. But his mother said, "No; he is to be called John." They said to her, "None of your relatives has this name." Then they began motioning to his father to find out what name he wanted to give him. He asked for a writing tablet and wrote, "His name is John." And all of them were amazed. Immediately his mouth was opened and his tongue freed, and he began to speak, praising God. Fear came over all their neighbors, and all these things were talked about throughout the entire hill country of Judea.

All who heard them pondered them and said, "What then will this child become?" For, indeed, the hand of the Lord was with him.

Then his father Zechariah was filled with the Holy Spirit and spoke this prophecy:

"Blessed be the Lord God of Israel,
> *for he has looked favorably on his people and redeemed them.*
He has raised up a mighty savior for us
> *in the house of his servant David,*
as he spoke through the mouth of his holy prophets from of old,
> *that we would be saved from our enemies and from the hand of all who hate us.*
Thus he has shown the mercy promised to our ancestors,
> *and has remembered his holy covenant,*
the oath that he swore to our ancestor Abraham,
> *to grant us that we, being rescued from the hands of our enemies,*
might serve him without fear, in holiness and righteousness
> *before him all our days.*
And you, child, will be called the prophet of the Most High;
> *for you will go before the Lord to prepare his ways,*
to give knowledge of salvation to his people
> *by the forgiveness of their sins.*
By the tender mercy of our God,
> *the dawn from on high will break upon us,*
to give light to those who sit in darkness and in the shadow of death,
> *to guide our feet into the way of peace."*

The child grew and became strong in spirit, and he was in the wilderness until the day he appeared publicly to Israel. (1:57–80)

Journey to Bethlehem and Birth of Jesus in a Stable

In those days a decree went out from Emperor Augustus that all the world should be registered. This was the first registration and was taken while Quirinius was governor of Syria. All went to their own towns to be registered. Joseph also went from the town of Nazareth in Galilee to Judea, to the city of David called Bethlehem, because he was descended from the house and family of David. He went to be registered with Mary, to whom he was engaged and who was expecting a child. While they were there, the time came for her to deliver her child. And she gave birth to her firstborn son and wrapped him in bands of cloth, and laid him in a manger, because there was no place for them in the inn. (2:1–7)

Announcement of Jesus's Birth by Angels

In that region there were shepherds living in the fields, keeping watch over their flock by night. Then an angel of the Lord stood before them, and the glory of the Lord shone around them, and they were terrified. But the angel said to them, "Do not be afraid; for see—I am bringing you good news of great joy for all the people: to you is born this day in the city of David a Savior, who is the Messiah, the Lord. This will be a sign for you: you will find a child wrapped in bands of cloth and lying in a manger." And suddenly there was with the angel a multitude of the heavenly host, praising God and saying,

"Glory to God in the highest heaven,
and on earth peace among those whom he favors!"

When the angels had left them and gone into heaven, the shepherds said to one another, "Let us go now to Bethlehem and see this thing that has taken place, which the Lord has made known to us." So they went with haste and found Mary and Joseph, and the child lying in the manger. When they saw this, they made known what had been told them about this child; and all who heard it were amazed at what the shepherds told them. But Mary treasured all these words and pondered them in her heart. The shepherds returned, glorifying and praising God for all they had heard and seen, as it had been told them. (2:8–20)

Circumcision of Jesus

After eight days had passed, it was time to circumcise the child; and he was called Jesus, the name given by the angel before he was conceived in the womb. (2:21)

Presentation of Jesus in the Temple and Hymn (the Nunc Dimittis)

When the time came for their purification according to the law of Moses, they brought him up to Jerusalem to present him to the Lord (as it is written in the law of the Lord, "Every firstborn male shall be designated as holy to the Lord"), and they offered a sacrifice according to what is stated in the law of the Lord, "a pair of turtle-doves or two young pigeons."

Now there was a man in Jerusalem whose name was Simeon; this man was righteous and devout, looking forward to the consolation of Israel, and the Holy Spirit rested on him. It had been revealed to him by the Holy Spirit that he would not see death before he had seen the Lord's Messiah. Guided by the Spirit, Simeon came into the temple; and when the parents brought in the child Jesus, to do for him what was customary under the law, Simeon took him in his arms and praised God, saying,

> *"Master, now you are dismissing your servant in peace,*
>   *according to your word;*
> *for my eyes have seen your salvation,*
>   *which you have prepared in the presence of all peoples,*
> *a light for revelation to the Gentiles*
>   *and for glory to your people Israel."*

And the child's father and mother were amazed at what was being said about him. Then Simeon blessed them and said to his mother Mary, "This child is destined for the falling and the rising of many in Israel, and to be a sign that will be opposed so that the inner thoughts of many will be revealed—and a sword will pierce your own soul too."

There was also a prophet, Anna the daughter of Phanuel, of the tribe of Asher. She was of a great age, having lived with her husband seven years after her marriage, then as a widow to the age of eighty-four. She never left the temple but worshiped there with fasting and prayer night and day. At that moment she came, and began to praise God and to speak about the child to all who were looking for the redemption of Jerusalem.

When they had finished everything required by the law of the Lord, they returned to Galilee, to their own town of Nazareth. (2:22–39)

Jesus at Age Twelve in the Temple

The child grew and became strong, filled with wisdom; and the favor of God was upon him.

Now every year his parents went to Jerusalem for the festival of the Passover. And when he was twelve years old, they went up as usual for the festival. When the festival was ended and they started to return, the boy Jesus stayed behind in Jerusalem, but his parents did not know it. Assuming that he was in the group of travelers, they went a day's journey. Then they started to look for him among their relatives and friends. When they did not find him, they returned to Jerusalem to search for him. After three days they found him in the temple, sitting among the teachers, listening to them and asking them questions. And all who heard him were amazed at his understanding and his answers. When his parents saw him they were astonished; and his mother said to him, "Child, why have you treated us like this? Look, your father and I have been searching for you in great anxiety." He said to them, "Why were you searching for me? Did you not know that I must be in my Father's house?" But they did not understand what he said to them. Then he went down with them and came to Nazareth, and was obedient to them. His mother treasured all these things in her heart.

And Jesus increased in wisdom and in years, and in divine and human favor. (2:40–52)

FEATURES OF A PAGEANT BASED ON LUKE

First, much of the pageant would be about the parents of John the Baptizer, Zechariah and Elizabeth. They appear in forty-three verses, more than half of Luke's first chapter (in Matthew's birth story, there is no mention of John or his parents).

Elizabeth and Zechariah are childless, and both are very old. In this, they are like Abraham and Sarah in the Old Testament, the ancestors of Israel. But then, as with Abraham and Sarah, Elizabeth conceives in her old age. The child, known to history as John the Baptizer, will be like Elijah, one of the greatest prophets of ancient Israel and one who, many Jews believed, would return as the predecessor, the forerunner, of the kingdom of God. Elizabeth appears in the story again when Mary (now pregnant with Jesus) visits her.

A second feature of a pageant based on Luke is that women play much more prominent roles. We have just mentioned Elizabeth. And Mary's role is much greater than in Matthew, where she is a completely passive figure, neither speaking nor receiving any revelation. For much of Luke's birth story, Mary is the central character. Indeed, Joseph is almost invisible in Luke, in sharp contrast to Matthew. Luke's pageant also has a third woman, the eighty-four-year-old prophet Anna, who "began to praise God and to speak about the child to all who were looking for the redemption of Jerusalem" (2:38).

Music would constitute a third feature of Luke's pageant— lots of it. His story has three hymns, or canticles. Though Luke does not call them "hymns," they have been sung by Christians for centuries and may well have originated as hymns. The first two (the Benedictus, sung by Zechariah, and the Magnificat, sung by Mary) are longer, and the third (the Nunc Dimittis, sung by Simeon) is shorter. Because each is sung by an individual, we might imagine them as three arias. In addition to these three arias, a brief song is sung by a chorus of angels in the night sky to stunned shepherds below: "Glory to God in the highest heaven, and on earth peace among those whom he favors!" (2:14).

A fourth feature of Luke's pageant is that it would include the most familiar part of the Christmas story (2:1–20). Its opening words are fixed in the memories of many: "In those days a decree went out from Emperor Augustus that all the world should be registered." Joseph and Mary make the journey from Nazareth to Bethlehem, where Jesus is born in a stable and placed in a manger. Then to shepherds "keeping watch over their flock by night" an angel of the Lord appears and proclaims, "To you is born this day in the city of David a Savior who is the Messiah, the Lord."

And, as a final feature, Luke's pageant would go on considerably longer than one based on Matthew. We refer not simply to the greater number of verses in Luke, but the extension of his story into Jesus's infancy and youth. Luke narrates the circumcision of Jesus when he was eight days old and his presentation in the temple when he was about forty days old, where he was acclaimed by Simeon and Anna. Luke's pageant would conclude with Jesus at age twelve in Jerusalem amazing the teachers in the temple with his wisdom.

THE RICHNESS OF TWO STORIES

As we complete our description of the Christmas pageant that would result from each gospel, we underline our primary purpose for doing so. Our major point is very simple: these are very different stories. Of course, they share some things in common: the names of Jesus's parents, his birth in Bethlehem near the end of the reign of Herod the Great, and his conception by the Spirit of God. Yet these points of commonality are embedded in two very different narratives.

Most often, as we noted at the beginning of this chapter, we do not hear the stories of the first Christmas as whole and distinct narratives. Rather, we hear them through filters. One common filter is "harmonizing" them, either by combining them into one story or preferring one version and ignoring contradictions from the other. Another common filter is hearing them through later tradition. We provide an example of each.

What was the home of Mary and Joseph before Jesus was born? Where did they live? Most people would answer: Nazareth. In Luke's story, Mary and Joseph live in Nazareth in Galilee, where Mary has become pregnant by the Spirit. When it is almost time for her to give birth, she and Joseph journey from Nazareth to Bethlehem in Judea, where there is no room in the inn, and so Jesus is born in a stable and placed in a manger. But in Matthew, Mary and Joseph live not in Nazareth, but in Bethlehem, where Jesus is born at home. Nazareth becomes their home only after they return from Egypt after Herod's death. They move to Nazareth because the new ruler of Judea, Herod's son Archelaus, is as dangerous as his father was.

These two living and travel patterns are very different and do not lend themselves to combination. Because Luke's nativity story is the longer one replete with colorful details, most people are familiar with the Nazareth to Bethlehem to Nazareth pattern. The Bethlehem to Egypt to Nazareth pattern in Matthew is largely ignored.

As an example of a filter of tradition, who brought gifts of gold, frankincense, and myrrh to the infant Jesus? Many would answer: three kings from the East, as in the well-known Christmas carol "We Three Kings of Orient Are." But Matthew's story does not refer to kings. Instead, Matthew speaks of wise men, *magi,* from the East. And how many wise men were there? Matthew does not tell us how many—only that they brought three gifts. The notion that there were *three* and that they were *kings* is a much later tradition.

These examples are not meant as a condescending comment about how little people really know about these stories. Rather, they suggest the need to read and hear these stories anew, seeking to see them in their rich distinctiveness.

It is not impossible to harmonize them. Indeed, they have been harmonized for most of Christian history, their stories combined or their differences set aside or not seen. There is nothing intrinsically wrong with harmonizing, no point in condemning Christmas pageants or artistic or musical renditions that do so. But there is great value in recognizing their differences and reading them as separate stories. Reading each as a separate narrative and paying attention to the details of the texts enriches these stories and adds greatly to their power. Meaning grows larger, not smaller.

To avoid a possible misunderstanding, recognizing the differences is not about pointing out "contradictions," as debunkers of the stories often do. In their minds, the differences mean that the stories are fabrications, made-up tales unworthy of serious attention. That is not our point at all. Rather, paying attention to the distinctiveness and details of the nativity stories is how we enter into the possibility of understanding what they meant in the first century and might still mean for communities of faith today.

Though this approach leads to results that are surprising to some, it is hardly radical. To put it simply, our approach to these stories is: "Read the texts—and pay attention." Doing so should be the basis for all serious reading of the Bible.

CHAPTER TWO

PARABLES AS OVERTURES

I n this chapter, we begin by reporting how the stories of the first Christmas are seen within contemporary biblical scholarship. We then turn to important questions. What kind of stories are theses? What is their purpose, their function? And how is each connected to the gospel that it introduces?

THE NATIVITY STORIES IN EARLY CHRISTIANITY

A consensus of mainstream biblical scholarship sees the stories as relatively late in the development of early Christianity. Matthew and Luke were most likely written in the last two decades of the first century, in the 80s or 90s CE. They are not the earliest Christian writings. That honor belongs to the genuine letters of Paul, written in the decade of the 50s, and to the gospel of Mark, written around the year 70.

In Mark and Paul, there is no mention of an extraordinary birth of Jesus. Mark begins his gospel with Jesus as an adult; his birth is not mentioned at all. Though Paul refers to his birth twice, he does not mention that it was exceptional. In Romans 1:3, Jesus was "descended from David according to the flesh." In Galatians 4:4, Jesus was "born of a woman, born under the law." But there is no hint that his birth was unusual. Finally, we note that the gospel of John, though later than both Mark and Paul and probably later than Matthew and Luke, does not have a birth story either.

From this scholarly consensus about the dating of Matthew and Luke in relation to earlier Christian writings flows an obvious inference: stories of Jesus's birth were not of major importance to earliest Christianity. Mark wrote a gospel without referring to Jesus's birth, as John later did. Though the end of Jesus's life—his crucifixion and resurrection—are utterly central to Paul, he says nothing about how his life began.

From this inference flows a second highly probable inference: the reason that references to a special birth do not appear in the earliest Christian writings is either because the stories did not yet exist or because they were still in the process of formation. In either case, these stories are relatively late, not part of the earliest Christian tradition about Jesus.

Fact, Fable, or Parable?

We turn now to crucial questions for hearing and interpreting the stories of the first Christmas. What kind of stories are these? What is their purpose? What did their authors intend them to be? What is their literary genre?

A recent television special on the birth of Jesus posed the question this way: are these stories fact or fable? For many people, Christians and non-Christians alike, these are the two choices. Either these stories report events that happened, or they are no better than fables. For most people today, fables do not matter much. They might be entertaining for children, but need not be taken seriously.

Thus it is important to realize that there is a third option that moves beyond the choices of fact or fable. This book is based on the third option. We see the nativity stories as neither fact nor fable, but as parables and overtures. Later in this chapter we describe what it means to see them this way. But first we explain how the options of fact or fable arose.

The issue of the factuality of the birth stories is recent, the product of the last few hundred years. In earlier centuries, their factuality was not a concern for Christians. Rather, the truth of these stories (including their factual truth) was taken for granted. Their truth, and the truth of the Bible as whole, was part of conventional wisdom in Christian areas of the world. It was part of "what everybody knew." Believing them to be true (including factually true) was effortless. Nobody worried about whether they were factually true. All of the interpretive focus was on their meaning.

The same was true of the early chapters of Genesis with the stories of creation, the Garden of Eden, Adam and Eve, Noah and the great flood, and the tower of Babel. Premodern Christians saw them as stories of the way things happened. There was no reason for them to think otherwise. It didn't take faith to believe in them, just as it didn't take faith to believe in the factuality of the nativity stories.

Many of us have a childhood memory of hearing the birth stories this way. Most of us who grew up Christian took their factuality for granted when we were young children, just as people in the premodern Christian world did. We heard them in an early childhood state of mind known as "precritical naïveté." In this stage, we take it for granted that whatever the significant authority figures in our life regard as true is indeed true. So it was for both of us. Whether these stories were factual was not an issue. Indeed, Marcus can remember as a child looking for the star of Bethlehem on Christmas Eve, thinking that perhaps it appeared every year on the night of Jesus's birth.

THE IMPACT OF THE ENLIGHTENMENT

But this precritical way of seeing the birth stories has become impossible in the modern world, for Christians and non-Christians alike. The reason is the impact of the Enlightenment, which began in the seventeenth century with the emergence of modern science and scientific ways of knowing. It generated a new period of Western cultural history commonly called "modernity." Modernity's effect on the world has been enormous; its technological achievements are the most obvious result.

Of greatest importance for our purposes, modernity has pervasively affected how modern people think. It produced what has been called the "modern mind," a mind-set that shapes all of our thinking. The Enlightenment generated an understanding of truth and reality very different from that in the premodern world. In philosophical terms, it generated a new *epistemology* and a new *ontology*. The former focuses on "How do we know?" and "What is true?" The latter focuses on "What is real?" and "What is possible?"

To begin with the first, the Enlightenment led many people to think that truth and factuality are the same. Its mind-set was (and is) concerned with the distinction between truth and superstition, truth and fable, truth and traditional authority, truth and belief. The primary basis for the distinction is the modern scientific way of knowing, with its emphasis on experimentation and verification.

In the minds of many people, this has led to the notion that truth is what can be verified—and what can be verified, of course, are "facts." The contemporary scholar of religion Huston Smith calls this notion "fact fundamentalism," even as he rejects it. According to this way of thinking, if something isn't factual, it isn't true.

Fact fundamentalism has impacted Christians as well as those who are skeptical of religion in general and Christianity in particular. Many in both groups agree that a statement or story is true only if it is factual. Among American Christians, this is a major reason why at least half affirm a literal-factual understanding of the Genesis stories of creation and of the Bible as a whole, including the birth stories. In their minds, if these stories aren't factual, then they are not true, and the Bible itself is not true. Christian biblical literalism is about biblical factuality, and it is rooted in fact fundamentalism. As such, it is not ancient, but a product of the recent past.

The Enlightenment had an additional effect. The modern mind is shaped not only by fact fundamentalism, but by a worldview—an image of reality, of what is real and what is possible, a big picture of "the way things are." With the Enlightenment came a worldview very different from premodern worldviews, a new ontology. Within the modern worldview, what is indubitably real is the space-time universe of matter and energy, operating in accord with natural laws of cause and effect.

This worldview, this vision of what is real and what is possible, has shaped everybody who lives in the modern world, even those who reject it. We internalize it simply by growing up in the modern world; it is what we are socialized into. It affects believers and nonbelievers alike.

Its view of what is real and what is possible makes the central claims of religion questionable. Within this framework, what happens to claims about a nonmaterial reality, about spiritual reality, about God? Prior to the Enlightenment, the reality of God was taken for granted; it didn't require "belief." Indeed, God was seen as "more real" than the world. But the Enlightenment worldview reverses this. This world—the space-time universe of matter and energy—is what seems unmistakably real, and the reality of God has become questionable.

Thus the modern worldview engenders skepticism about stories of spectacular events such as those narrated in the nativity stories. Do things like this ever happen—supernatural interventions, virgin births, special stars, angelic visitations? At the same time that truth became identified with factuality, the factuality of the birth stories was called into question by the modern worldview.

In this cultural context, the choice of seeing the birth stories as fact or fable emerged. Many find their factuality difficult and even impossible to believe. Things like those reported in the stories don't happen. Some may also be aware that stories of divine conceptions are, if not a dime a dozen, relatively common in the ancient world. This is the way ancient people spoke about figures of great importance. And some may also point to the differences in the birth stories as yet another reason to see them as not factual, and thus not true.

CHRISTIAN RESPONSES

Christians have responded in more than one way to the impact of the Enlightenment on the stories of the first Christmas. The most publicly visible form of Christianity insists on their factuality, in spite of the doubts generated by the modern worldview. This response, which we call "conscious literalism" or "insistent literalism," is very different from the taken-for-granted literalism of our premodern ancestors and from the precritical naïveté of childhood. Conscious literalists are aware that the events in these stories are hard to believe and yet insist, with varying degrees of intensity, that they are factual. Conscious literalism is modern, grounded in the fact fundamentalism of the Enlightenment.

These Christians counter the notion that spectacular events like those in the stories don't happen by affirming that they are supernatural interventions by God. Often they claim that because God is all-powerful, God can do anything, and that doubting the factuality of these stories is to doubt the power of God. In their judgment, skepticism flows from lack of faith.

In conservative Christian circles, a fairly common theological orientation reinforces a literal-factual interpretation of the virgin birth: if Jesus wasn't conceived by the Holy Spirit and born of a virgin, then he isn't really the Son of God. If he had a human father, he's just like us, not really special. For them, Jesus's status as divine is at stake. "Do you believe that Jesus was born of a virgin?" becomes a test of faith, a test of Christian orthodoxy.

For some, there is a second theological factor, the notion of "original sin." One understanding of "original sin" sees it as transmitted from generation to generation through sexual intercourse. Christians who see it this way think that if Jesus was conceived in the normal human way, he would have inherited original sin and thus could not be the sinless sacrifice that atones for the sins of humankind. For them, what is at stake in the virgin birth is nothing less than the saving significance of Jesus's death.

For these Christians, the factuality of the virgin birth and the nativity stories matters a great deal. Defending them against the thought that they might be fables is imperative. But note that both biblical literalists and modern skeptics agree: if these stories aren't factual, they aren't true. And if they aren't factual, then the Bible and Christianity aren't true.

But there are also many Christians who reject the notion that the truth of Christianity is dependent upon a factual understanding of these stories. Like the skeptics, they wonder whether virginal conceptions ever happen. Some are aware of other problems with understanding the nativity stories factually. But uncertainty about the stories does not lead to a skeptical rejection of the Bible and Christianity. For them, that is not at stake.

Yet many of these Christians are unsure about what to make of the birth stories. If they're not factual, what are they? What is the alternative? Are they simply the imaginative product of early Christians, with no more significance than other ancient fables? Or is there an alternative way of seeing them?

THE BIRTH STORIES AS PARABLE

To say the obvious, deciding how to read these stories involves an interpretive decision. This is true even when they are read literally and factually; the stories do not come with a footnote that says, "These are factually true stories." There is no non-interpretive way of reading them. Every way of reading them involves an interpretive decision about the kind of stories they are. Making an interpretive decision means asking: what has each way of interpreting them got going for it? How adequately does it account for what we see when we pay attention to what is in the text?

To state our interpretive decision, we best understand the nativity stories and their meanings by treating them as neither fact nor fable, but as *parable*. Parable is a form of speech, just as poetry is a form of speech. It is a way of using language.

The model for our understanding of the nativity stories as parable is the parables of Jesus. They were his most distinctive style of teaching. More parables are attributed to Jesus than to any other figure in the Jewish tradition. The most famous of them—the prodigal son and the good Samaritan—are as well known among Christians as the nativity stories. Almost as well known are parables like the workers in the vineyard, the unmerciful servant, the wicked tenants, the shepherd and the lost sheep, and the woman and the lost coin.

Parabolic Truth

By definition, a parable is a narrative, a story. As in all stories, something happens. This is true even in the shortest of Jesus's parables: a man discovers buried treasure in a field, a merchant searches for fine pearls, a woman puts leaven in flour, a woman searches for a lost coin. People do things in parables; something happens. But no one worries about whether the events in parabolic narratives are factual. Parable as a form of language is about meaning, not factuality. The meaning of a parable—its parabolic truth—does not depend upon its factuality.

Parables are thus a form of metaphorical language. The metaphorical meaning of language is its "more-than-literal" meaning, the capacity of language to carry a surplus of meaning. A parable is a narrative metaphor, a metaphorical narrative, whose truth lies in its meaning.

All Christians agree about this. They see Jesus's parables as meaning-filled and truth-filled, as meaningful and truthful stories. Yet no Christian we know of worries about whether the parables are factual. Everybody agrees that Jesus made them up. To think that they are reports of factual events or that their truth depends on their factuality is to misunderstand them and their purpose.

Imagine somebody wanting to argue that the parables of Jesus *do* report factual history and that their truth depends upon that. That person says there really had to have been a Samaritan who compassionately came to the aid of a victim of violent robbery on the road from Jerusalem to Jericho, or else the story isn't true and shouldn't be taken seriously. If it's not fact, it's fable. Everybody would say, "No, that's not the point." Suppose our hypothetical factualist were to continue by saying, "But he's just making this stuff up!" Everybody would say, "You're just not getting it—you are debating historicity and avoiding the question of meaning," or, much less politely, in language we would never use, "It's a parable, dummy."

Our point is obvious: the parables of Jesus matter and they are truthful even though they're not factual, even though they're "made-up" stories. For those who have ears to hear, they are full of truth. The application to the birth stories is equally obvious. To see these stories as parables means that their meaning and truth do not depend on their factuality. Indeed, being concerned with their factuality risks missing their meaning and truth, just as arguing for a real good Samaritan would miss the point. The truth of parabolic language does not depend on its factuality.

Jesus told parables about God and the advent of God, the coming of God's kingdom. His followers told parables about Jesus and his advent, the coming of the bearer of God's kingdom. In this sense, we see the birth stories as parables about Jesus. We focus on their more-than-literal, more-than-factual meanings. To see these stories as parabolic or metaphorical narratives does not require denying their factuality. It simply sets that question aside. A parabolic approach means, "Believe whatever you want about whether the stories are factual— now, let's talk about what these stories *mean.*" Meaning, not factuality, is emphasized.

A Historical and Parabolic Approach

The parabolic approach needs to be combined with a historical approach, and so we add a second adjective to our way of seeing the birth stories. By "historical," we do not mean factual, even as we recognize that that is one of the meanings people associate with the word in our time. When people ask about a story, "Is that historical?" they mean, "Did that happen? Is that factual?"

But this is not what we mean. Rather, a historical approach to these stories means setting these ancient parables in their first-century context. Just as the parables of Jesus become powerfully meaningful in their first-century context, so also do early Christian stories about Jesus. A historical approach means "ancient text in ancient context." What did these stories mean for the Christian communities that told them near the end of the first century?

This historical-parabolic or historical-metaphorical approach to the birth stories is shared by the vast majority of contemporary mainstream scholars. Moreover, it has a broader application to biblical narratives generally: it is always the more-than-literal, the more-than-factual meaning of biblical stories that matters most. That is why they were told again and again, because of their surplus of meaning.

Seeing the birth stories as parabolic narratives provides a way of moving beyond the fractious and fruitless "fact or fable" conflict, marked by endless assertion and counterassertion: "They're factually true." "No, they aren't." "Yes, they are." "No, they're not." When their factuality is emphasized, the issue becomes, "Do I believe them or not?" Did these events, including especially the spectacular ones, actually happen? The debate is not only fruitless, but a distraction, for it shifts attention away from the truly important question: what do these stories mean? Quite apart from whether they happened, what did they and do they *mean*?

Parables as Subversive Stories

A second feature of the parables of Jesus adds to our model for interpreting the birth stories. In addition to providing a way of seeing that parabolic language can be true independently of factuality, his parables were subversive stories.

They subverted conventional ways of seeing life and God. They undermined a "world," meaning a taken-for-granted way of seeing "the way things are." Jesus's parables invited his hearers into a different way of seeing how things are and how we might live. As invitations to see differently, they were subversive. Indeed, perhaps seeing differently is the foundation of subversion.

Like his parables, the birth stories are subversive. They subverted the "world" in which Jesus and early Christianity lived. As stories told by his followers late in the first century, they are part of their testimony, their witness, to the significance that Jesus had come to have for them. That significance had at its center a different vision of life, a vision they got from Jesus—from his teaching, his public activity, and his life, death, and vindication by God. The vision was embodied in Jesus, incarnate in Jesus.

And just as Jesus told subversive stories about God, his followers told subversive stories about Jesus. The gospels are full of them. The birth stories are among them. To illustrate, we here simply name, without detailed exposition, some of the themes we develop at greater length in the rest of this book:

- Who is the "King of the Jews"? That was Herod the Great's title, but Matthew's story tells us Herod was more like Pharaoh, the lord of Egypt, the lord of bondage and oppression, violence and brutality. And his son was no better. Rather, Jesus is the true King of the Jews. And the rulers of his world sought to destroy him.

- Who is the Son of God, Lord, savior of the world, and the one who brings peace on earth? Within Roman imperial theology, the emperor, Caesar, was all of these. No, Luke's story says, that status and those titles belong to Jesus. He—not the emperor—is the embodiment of God's will for the earth.

- Who is the light of the world? The emperor, son of Apollo, the god of light and reason and imperial order? Or is Jesus, who was executed by empire, the light in the darkness, the true light to whom the wise of this world are drawn?

- Where do we find the fulfillment of God's dream for Israel and humanity? In the way things are now? Or only beyond death? Or in a very different world this side of death?

The birth stories subvert the dominant consciousness of the first-century world as well as our own. Jesus's followers learned well how to tell subversive stories, and presumably they learned the gift from him.

Thus, in our considered judgment, Matthew 1–2 and Luke 1–2 contain, and were intended to contain, minimal historical information—probably just the three items that Jesus was a historical figure whose parents were Mary and Joseph and whose home was at Nazareth in Galilee. But, in this book, we are not interested in a long string of negatives or a dreary list of what did not happen. Rather, the realization of how little is historical in these stories points to parabolic meaning. It is never, ever enough to say that some event did not happen without asking, why, then, did Matthew or Luke create it? And that is always a question of meaning.

PARABOLIC OVERTURES

We turn next to a second major and equally important facet of those two Christmas stories. They are not just parables, but overtures, parabolic overtures—each to its respective gospel. In other words, Matthew 1–2 is a miniature version of the succeeding Matthew 3–28, and Luke 1–2 is a miniature version of Luke 3–24. Each is its own gospel in miniature and microcosm. But, since Matthew and Luke have quite different gospels, they must also have quite different overtures.

What exactly is an overture? It is the opening part (French *ouverture*) of a work that serves as summary, synthesis, metaphor, or symbol of the whole. We all recognize overtures quite easily when we are dealing with classical operas or popular musicals. But it may be harder to grasp an overture in a literary text. But here is a good example even in a historical study.

Barbara Tuchman's *The Guns of August* is a magnificent history of the outbreak of World War I. Her 1962 Pulitzer Prize winner has three major parts entitled "Plans," "Outbreak," and "Battle." But her first chapter precedes those three sections and is entitled "A Funeral." She describes how the crowned heads of Europe gathered in London for the burial of Edward VII. She is both starting her story by describing what actually happened that May morning in 1910 and symbolizing the burial of the old European order that would follow it between 1914 and 1918 as millions died, dynasties fell, and thrones were emptied forever. A European funeral is the most appropriate overture for that "brutal, mud-filled, murderous insanity known as the Western Front that was to last for four more years."[1] A European burial is the most appropriate overture for a war in which "the known dead per capita of population were 1 to 28 in France, 1 to 32 in Germany, 1 to 57 for England and 1 to 107 for Russia."[2] Her section entitled "A Funeral" is not just a first chapter; it is a profoundly appropriate overture. It is all that follows in miniature and microcosm.

Furthermore, once each birth story is understood properly as a parabolic overture, the problem of Jesus's "missing years" disappears completely. It is not that we have detailed historical information about the genealogy, conception, birth, and infancy of Jesus, and then a yawning gap opens up until his public life begins around the age of thirty. It is rather that all the years are missing until the story begins—as it does in all four gospels—with John's baptism of Jesus.

THE BIBLE AS "OLD" AND "NEW" TESTAMENT

Before we get into the separate overtures in Matthew 1–2 and Luke 1–2, we look at one common impulse behind them both. And this concerns the New Testament as the climactic consummation—and never the simple replacement—of the Old Testament in the Christian Bible.

First, two powerful streams of interpretation flowed out from the common Jewish biblical tradition during that terrible first century CE. Each would eventually claim exclusive rights to its own understanding of the past as the only authentic vision for the future. We now name those two streams as Judaism and Christianity, and in this book, to change the metaphor, we think of them as twin daughters born in a hard and difficult delivery for their mother. Judaism and Christianity are, for us, a double covenant and, no matter how each has disputed the other's dignity and integrity throughout the centuries, we hold them as fully and equally valid before God.

Second, our Christian Bible is divided into an Old Testament and a New Testament, terms that are in no way derogatory to that common biblical matrix. For us moderns the "old" is often considered useless and the "new" is what is important and significant. For the ancients, it was, rather, the opposite. The "old" was the tried and true, while the "new" was often mistrusted and suspected. Greeks and Romans, for example, may have mocked Judaism, but at least they respected its antiquity.

When we speak about the New Testament in this book, then, we do not think of it as having superceded the Old Testament, but having brought it to one of its two fulfillments. The other fulfillment, of course, is in the Mishnah and Talmuds of Judaism. In Jeremiah 31:31, for example, God promised "a new covenant," or testament, which is no more and no less than the old covenant re-*new*-ed—and renewed differently for Jews and Christians.

Third, there is one fundamental constitutive element common to the Christmas stories in Matthew and Luke. Both Matthew 1–2 and Luke 1–2 insist that the birth of Jesus is the glorious completion and perfection of the tradition into which he was born. He is, for them, the magnificent and climactic completion of the hope and fears of his people, his tradition, and his homeland.

Fourth, based on that common faith in Jesus as the fulfillment and consummation rather than replacement and abandonment of Israel, each overture goes its own very individual way. In the rest of this chapter, we show how Matthew and Luke create overtures that depict their gospels in miniature. And, as we shall see, that overture-as-microcosm represents the gospel-as-macrocosm with regard to both content and format.

MATTHEW'S CHRISTMAS STORY AS OVERTURE

We begin with Matthew 1–2 as an overture to Matthew 3–28. The major theme is a very basic parallel between Jesus and Moses, an interpretation of Jesus as the new—that is, re-*new*ed—Moses.

First of all, what is the most obvious parallel between the birth of Jesus in Matthew 1–2 in the New Testament and the birth of Moses in Exodus 1–2 of the Old Testament? It is surely that, in both cases, an evil ruler—Herod in Matthew 1–2, Pharaoh in Exodus 1–2—plots to kill all the newly born Jewish males and thereby endangers the life of the predestined child, who is only saved by divine intervention and heavenly protection.

Even if we do not catch that parallel immediately, anyone in the first century CE who knew the biblical tradition and the importance of Moses in it would see it as the most striking parallel between the birth story of Jesus in Matthew 1–2 and that of Moses in Exodus 1–2. It would scream to those Jews as it should to us Christians as loudly as a giant newspaper headline:

EVIL RULER SLAUGHTERS MALE INFANTS
PREDESTINED CHILD ESCAPES

From the very beginning of his life, therefore, Jesus was already the new Moses and Herod was the new Pharaoh. And that is our major clue to Matthew's intention in his Christmas story as overture to his gospel.

Next, focus on these twin items in that overture. Matthew moves the plot of his Christmas story as gospel overture by *five* divine dreams and *five* scriptural fulfillments. The plot and action of Matthew's birth story proceed by a series of divine interventions and instructions communicated in dreams:

1. *To Joseph:* "An angel of the Lord appeared to him in a dream and said, 'Joseph, son of David, do not be afraid to take Mary as your wife, for the child conceived in her is from the Holy Spirit.'" (1:20)

2. *To the Magi:* "Having been warned in a dream not to return to Herod, they left for their own country by another road." (2:12)

3. *To Joseph:* "An angel of the Lord appeared to Joseph in a dream and said, 'Get up, take the child and his mother, and flee to Egypt.'" (2:13)

4. *To Joseph:* "An angel of the Lord suddenly appeared in a dream to Joseph in Egypt and said, 'Get up, take the child and his mother, and go to the land of Israel, for those who were seeking the child's life are dead.'" (2:19–20)

5. *To Joseph:* "But when he heard that Archelaus was ruling over Judea in place of his father Herod, he was afraid to go there. And after being warned in a dream, he went away to the district of Galilee." (2:22)

There are five such dreams, and after each one the directive is immediately obeyed. In other words, the entire progression of the plot is under fivefold divine control. And, except for once for the Magi, all the dreams are for Joseph.

There are also a series of prophetic fulfillments and, once again, there are five such explicit references:

1. *On Mary's virginal conception:* "All this took place to fulfill what had been spoken by the Lord through the prophet: 'Look, the virgin shall conceive and bear a son, and they shall name him Emmanuel,' which means, 'God is with us.'" (1:22–23, citing Isa. 7:14)

2. *On the birthplace of the Messiah:* "Bethlehem of Judea; for so it has been written by the prophet: 'And you, Bethlehem, in the land of Judah, are by no means least among the rulers of Judah; for from you shall come a ruler who is to shepherd my people Israel.'" (2:5–6, citing Mic. 5:2; 2 Sam. 5:2)

3. *The departure of the Holy Family from Egypt:* "This was to fulfill what had been spoken by the Lord through the prophet, 'Out of Egypt I have called my son.'" (2:15, citing Hos. 11:1)

4. *After Herod's infanticide at Bethlehem:* "Then was fulfilled what had been spoken through the prophet Jeremiah: 'A voice was heard in Ramah, wailing and loud lamentation, Rachel weeping for her children; she refused to be consoled, because they are no more.'" (2:17–18, citing Jer. 31:15)

5. *On Nazareth:* "There he [Joseph] made his home in a town called Nazareth, so that what had been spoken through the prophets might be fulfilled, 'He [Jesus] will be called a Nazorean.'" (2:23, citation unknown)

In our world those prophetic fulfillments seem to be more and more of a stretch, to put it gently, and we treat this more fully in Chapter 8. But Matthew probably first decided that he needed precisely *five* prophetic fulfillments, went seeking them, and, lo and behold, found them. But why exactly did Matthew need *five* dreams and fulfillments and not any other number as the skeletal structure of his Christmas story? For the answer, we turn to Matthew's gospel, where Jesus is the new Moses.

First, that Jesus is Matthew's new Moses is immediately evident in what we—rather inappropriately—call the Sermon on the Mount in Matthew 5–7. It is actually, for Matthew, the *new* Moses giving a *new* Law from a *new* Mt. Sinai. It would be better to call it the "New Law from the New Mountain" rather than the Sermon on the Mount. There Matthew has Jesus as the new Moses proclaim: "Do not think that I have come to abolish

the law or the prophets; I have come not to abolish but to fulfill"
(5:17). That principle is then applied to six moral cases, and note
the repeated introduction to each one:

1. *On murder:* "You have heard that it was said to those of
   ancient times, 'You shall not murder.'. . . But I say to
   you that if you are angry with a brother or sister, you
   will be liable to judgment . . ." (5:21–26)

2. *On adultery:* "You have heard that it was said, 'You
   shall not commit adultery.'. . . But I say to you that
   everyone who looks at a woman with lust has already
   committed adultery . . ." (5:27–30)

3. *On divorce:* "It was also said, 'Whoever divorces his
   wife, let him give her a certificate of divorce.' But I say
   to you that anyone who divorces his wife . . . causes her
   to commit adultery . . ." (5:31–32)

4. *On oaths:* "Again, you have heard that it was said to
   those of ancient times, 'You shall not swear falsely.'. . .
   But I say to you, Do not swear at all . . ." (5:33–37)

5. *On nonviolence:* "You have heard that it was said, 'An
   eye for an eye.'. . . But I say to you, Do not resist an
   evildoer . . ." (5:38–42)

6. *On love for enemies:* "You have heard that it was said,
   'You shall . . . hate your enemy.'. . . But I say to you,
   Love your enemies . . ." (5:43–48)

You will notice that, in all those cases, the Law is fulfilled
by being made harder rather than easier; it is being radicalized
rather than liberalized. But that repeated refrain of "I say"
over against "was said" at the start of this, Jesus's inaugural

address, is the clearest indication that, for Matthew, Jesus is the new Moses and that the new law fulfills the old law by being even more ideally difficult than the earlier one was. But how does that parallelism create a need for *fives* in the overture?

The Torah, or Law of Moses, was contained most fully in the Pentateuch—(a term from the Greek for "Five Scrolls"). Those are the first five books of the Bible, the books of Genesis, Exodus, Numbers, Leviticus, and Deuteronomy. Therefore, Matthew structures his gospel so that Jesus gives *five* long addresses, as follows:

Book 1	Matthew 5–7	The Law Discourse (Sermon on the Mount)
Book 2	Matthew 10–11	The Missionary Discourse
Book 3	Matthew 13	The Parables Discourse
Book 4	Matthew 18–19	The Community Discourse
Book 5	Matthew 24–25	The Eschatological Discourse

Matthew 5–25 is a new five-book Pentateuch. Jesus as the new Moses is indicated throughout the entire text.

In summary, then, in both content and format, Matthew 1–2 is structured as an overture to Matthew 3–28; it is the gospel in miniature. And the theme in both is that Jesus is the new Moses.

LUKE'S CHRISTMAS STORY AS OVERTURE

Three important themes surface in Luke's overture as microcosm to his gospel as macrocosm: his emphasis on women, the marginalized, and the Holy Spirit.

Emphasis on Women. Luke sometimes emphasizes women themselves and sometimes balances a reference to a man with one to a woman. In his overture, the major focus is on Mary—

unlike in Matthew, where, as we saw in Chapter 1 and will see again in Chapter 5, it is very much on Joseph. Matthew accords righteousness only to Joseph (1:19), but in Luke John's parents, Zechariah and Elizabeth, are both "righteous before God" (1:6). The angel Gabriel informs Mary not only of her own, but also of Elizabeth's miraculous pregnancy (1:36). Mary visits Elizabeth and both speak prophetically (Elizabeth in 1:42–45, Mary in 1:46–55), just as Zechariah does (1:67–79). Elizabeth gives John his name, and Zechariah only confirms it (1:60–63). When Jesus is presented in the temple, he is greeted there by both a saintly man, the "righteous and devout" Simeon, and a saintly woman, the prophet Anna (2:25, 36). Finally, in the story about Jesus's coming-of-age, it is both parents—and not just the father—who are mentioned throughout the narrative (2:41–52; see Appendix 3).

After that emphasis on women and balance of female and male, we expect and find that Luke's gospel proper makes mention of women and balances female with male more than any of the other gospels. Here are some examples *found only in Luke:* the mother's only son at Nain, who is raised from death (7:11–16); the woman whose sins were forgiven (7:36–50); Martha and Mary, who host Jesus (10:38–42); the woman who addresses Jesus from the crowd (11:27–28); the crippled woman in the synagogue (13:10–16); the man with the lost sheep and the woman with the lost coin (15:4–7, 8–10); and the insistent widow (18:1–8). Finally, only Luke has all these named women who accompany Jesus:

> Soon afterward he went on through cities and villages, pro-claiming and bringing the good news of the kingdom of God. The twelve were with him, as well as some women who had been cured of evil spirits and infirmities: Mary,

called Magdalene, from whom seven demons had gone
out, and Joanna, the wife of Herod's steward Chuza, and
Susanna, and many others, who provided for them out
of their resources. (8:1–3)

Emphasis on the Marginalized. In Matthew, it is wise men
from the East who come to Jesus, but in Luke the angelic announcement of his birth is made to "shepherds living in the
fields, keeping watch over their flock by night" (2:8). As a class,
shepherds are even lower in the social order than peasants and
would qualify quite well as the "lowly" and the "hungry" of
Mary's hymn, the Magnificat (1:52–53).

This is another overture preparation for a theme very much
emphasized in Luke's gospel. He insists, again more than the
other gospels, on the obligations of the rich to the poor, the
outcasts, and the marginalized. Here are a few examples,
again found only in Luke. John the Baptizer urges that "whoever has two coats must share with anyone who has none;
and whoever has food must do likewise" (3:11). Jesus says in
Matthew, "Blessed are the poor in spirit" (5:3), but in Luke he
says, "Blessed are you who are poor" and "Woe to you who
are rich" (6:20, 24). Rich men are fools (12:16–21) or end up
in Hades (16:19–26). At the home of a Pharisee, Jesus advises:
"When you give a banquet, invite the poor, the crippled, the
lame, and the blind" (14:13). Finally, only Luke has the story
about Zacchaeus, the repentant tax collector and model Lukan
Christian, who announces: "Half of my possessions, Lord, I
will give to the poor; and if I have defrauded anyone of anything, I will pay back four times as much" (19:8).

Emphasis on the Holy Spirit. This third emphasis may be the
most important one from Luke's overture into not only his
gospel, but his Acts of the Apostles as well. Recall, of course,

that, for Luke, those books represented the first and second volumes of what was once his single, unified gospel.

In both the Matthean and Lukan overtures, angelic messengers announce that the child is from the Holy Spirit (Matt. 1:18–20; Luke 1:35). But Luke alone mentions the Holy Spirit coming on several other individuals in his overture:

On John: "He must never drink wine or strong drink; even before his birth he will be filled with the Holy Spirit." (1:15)

On Mary: "The angel said to her, 'The Holy Spirit will come upon you, and the power of the Most High will overshadow you; therefore the child to be born will be holy; he will be called Son of God.'" (1:35)

On Elizabeth: "When Elizabeth heard Mary's greeting, the child leaped in her womb. And Elizabeth was filled with the Holy Spirit." (1:41)

On Zechariah: "Then his father Zechariah was filled with the Holy Spirit." (1:67)

On Simeon: "Now there was a man in Jerusalem whose name was Simeon; this man was righteous and devout, looking forward to the consolation of Israel, and the Holy Spirit rested on him. It had been revealed to him by the Holy Spirit that he would not see death before he had seen the Lord's Messiah. Guided by the Spirit, Simeon came into the temple." (2:25–27)

Notice, by the way, that triple and therefore climactic repetition of the "Holy Spirit" in the case of Simeon in Luke 2:25–27 above.

That emphasis on the Holy Spirit in Luke's overture prepares us for the repeated emphasis on the Holy Spirit at the start of Jesus's public life in his gospel. That begins with the baptism of Jesus at the Jordan. In telling that story, Luke makes a double mention of the Holy Spirit—first in promise and then in advent—which is then picked up several times in the immediately following context:

> *The promise of the Holy Spirit:* "John answered all of them by saying, 'I baptize you with water; but one who is more powerful than I is coming; I am not worthy to untie the thong of his sandals. He will baptize you with the Holy Spirit and fire.'" (3:16)

> *The advent of the Holy Spirit:* "The Holy Spirit descended upon him [Jesus] in bodily form like a dove. And a voice came from heaven, 'You are my Son, the Beloved; with you I am well pleased.'" (3:22)

> *Jesus in the wilderness:* "Jesus, full of the Holy Spirit, returned from the Jordan and was led by the Spirit in the wilderness." (4:1)

> *The beginning of Jesus's ministry in Galilee:* "Jesus, filled with the power of the Spirit, returned to Galilee." (4:14)

> *Jesus's first address:* "The Spirit of the Lord is upon me, because he has anointed me to bring good news to the poor. He has sent me to proclaim release to the captives and recovery of sight to the blind, to let the oppressed go free." (4:18)

After that initial emphasis to indicate that Jesus's life is directed by the Holy Spirit, Luke does not pound on that point, but he ends the earthly life of Jesus with these words in 23:46: "Then Jesus, crying with a loud voice, said, 'Father, into your hands I commend my *spirit*.' Having said this, he breathed his last."

Furthermore, that emphasis on the guiding presence of the Holy Spirit is continued and even intensified in Luke's Acts of the Apostles. Watch, for example, how this second volume begins, like his first one, with the promise and advent of the Holy Spirit. In the gospel it was for the baptism of Jesus, but in Acts it is for the baptism of the church (our Feast of Pentecost):

Promise of the Holy Spirit: "John baptized with water, but you [the Twelve] will be baptized with the Holy Spirit not many days from now. . . . You will receive power when the Holy Spirit has come upon you; and you will be my witnesses in Jerusalem, in all Judea and Samaria, and to the ends of the earth. . . . And I [Peter] remembered the word of the Lord, how he had said, 'John baptized with water, but you will be baptized with the Holy Spirit.'" (1:5, 8; 11:16)

Advent of the Holy Spirit: "When the day of Pentecost had come, they were all together in one place. And suddenly from heaven there came a sound like the rush of a violent wind, and it filled the entire house where they were sitting. Divided tongues, as of fire, appeared among them, and a tongue rested on each of them. All of them were filled with the Holy Spirit and began to speak in other languages, as the Spirit gave them ability." (2:1–4)

And after that advent, the Holy Spirit is mentioned again and again as the guiding spirit of the early church. Watch, for example, how it guides Paul on his first (13:2–4), second (16:6–7), and final mission (19:21; 20:22–23).

The Power of Parabolic Overture

We began this section on the Christmas stories as overtures by giving one example of a literary overture, in that case a historical overture to a historical study. But one could also say that Barbara Tuchman's chapter entitled "A Funeral" is a parabolic overture to her entire book. The crowned heads of Europe gathered together around a casket was both a historical event and a parabolic prophecy. Here, to conclude this chapter, is another example—also in a historical study but also raising a historical event to prophetic overture.

In 1996 Stephen Ambrose published *Undaunted Courage: Meriwether Lewis, Thomas Jefferson, and the Opening of the American West*. Here is its opening paragraph:

> From the west-facing window of the room in which Meriwether was born on August 18, 1774, one could look out at Rockfish Gap, in the Blue Ridge Mountains, an opening to the West that invited exploration.[3]

We presume that statement to be historically correct and, maybe, that was the only window in the room that was available for mention. But a prophetic promise is surely intended by that first sentence. The words "opening" and "West" reverberate from the book's subtitle about the adult Lewis to that first perspective of the infant Lewis.

We propose that the Christmas stories, like those two usages, are primarily also parabolic overtures, but based on biblical tradition rather than on historical fact. Each is its gospel in miniature. When, therefore, Matthew 1–2 and Luke 1–2 are combined into a single Christmas story—for instance, in standard Christian imagination or the traditional Christian crèche—that story is the entire Christian gospel in miniature. Get it, and you get everything; miss it, and you miss all.

CHAPTER THREE

THE CONTEXT OF THE CHRISTMAS STORIES

What would you think of a book that started with the opener, "I am going to discuss Mahatma Gandhi as a Hindu saint, but I'll skip all that distracting stuff about British imperial India"? Or another with, "I am going to describe Dr. Martin Luther King Jr. as a Christian saint, but I'll get right to his biography and skip all that stuff about racism in America as background baggage"? You would know immediately that something is seriously wrong with those authors' presentations. In order, therefore, to emphasize situations where background is absolutely vital for understanding an individual's life, we distinguish between *background* and *context*.

THE CHALLENGE OF CONTEXT

You go to have a portrait taken. At the photographer's office, she shows you a rear-projection screen and a computerized projector with a hundred possible scenes. "What background," she asks, "do you want for your photograph? You can have a beach, a forest, a mountain, a glacier; you can have the White House, the Eiffel Tower, the Pyramids, or the Taj Mahal." Those scenes are mere *background,* which means that they will in no way interact with you. You will not be warm in front of a sunny beach as background, but you could get third-degree burns from one as context. You will not be cold in front of an icy glacier, but you could die of hypothermia from one as context. In other words, *context* interacts with you and so changes you even as you change it. That is why it cannot be omitted— because it is part of your present even as you are part of its future.

In this book we never speak of background and foreground, but of context and text. It is clear, however, that you cannot have con*text* without *text,* but it is not so immediately clear that you cannot have text without context. Often, therefore, we speak of *matrix* to designate the mutual creativity of text and context within a single interactive process. The term *matrix* indicates, for us, the necessary mutuality and reciprocity of text and context. Based on that principle, here is our question for this chapter. What is the contextual matrix that you must know to understand those Christmas stories as products of their first-century location?

The sequence of this chapter is this. First, we establish the clash between the kingdom of Rome and the kingdom of God as the context or matrix for our Christmas stories. Next, we look at the kingdom of Rome in all its overwhelming military, economic, political, and ideological power in the first century CE. Then, we look at the kingdom of God to see precisely how it differed from the kingdom of Rome. That difference needs to be carefully diagnosed, since the first-century emperor Caesar Augustus was entitled Lord, Son of God, Bringer of Peace, and Savior of the World. Yet those are the very titles that angelic messengers give to Jesus in the Christmas story of Luke: "Son of the Most High" and "Son of God" at Nazareth (1:32, 35); "Savior" and "Lord" as well as Bringer of "Peace" at Bethlehem (2:11, 14). Finally, lest all of this become too abstract, we look at the terrible brutality with which the kingdom of Rome struck Jesus's Galilean heartland around the very time of his birth.

The context or matrix of the Christmas stories has developed at least three layers—with each successive one always including its predecessor—across the two millennia of Christian interpretation. First of all, those Christmas stories were understood only *within Christianity,* within the New Testament as well as Christian legend and tradition, art and liturgy.

Next, and especially after World War II forced not just ecumenical respect but historical accuracy between contemporary Christianity and Judaism, that contextual matrix was expanded to interpret the Christmas stories *within Christianity within Judaism,* especially for that traumatic first century CE. Finally, and especially at the end of the twentieth and start of the twenty-first century, the full context for those Christmas stories is to see them *within Christianity within Judaism within the Roman Empire.* You will notice in that development, by the way, that *our* present is always and necessarily in creative interaction with *their* past.

We move now to consider the Christmas stories of Matthew 1–2 and Luke 1–2 in that last-mentioned context, that is, within Judaism as it strove with all its ancient and venerable traditions not just within, but also against, Roman imperial power. We begin with a metaphor taken from geology and applied to history.

We know that there are giant tectonic plates grinding ceaselessly against one another beneath the seemingly placid surface of our earth. Even when all is quiet along the surface of the San Andreas Fault, we know that in the depths beneath it the Pacific plate and the North American plate move slowly but relentlessly against one another. Think now of two huge tectonic plates grinding against one another in the depths below Mediterranean history in the first century CE. Their clash is the context for our Christmas stories in Matthew and Luke.

The grinding tectonics of the imperialism plate against the Judaism plate were as ancient as Pharaoh's millennium-old decree of genocide against the Israelites in Exodus 1–2 from the Old Testament. But that clash became much more obvious around the middle of the second century BCE, when the plate tectonics of imperialism versus Judaism became more precisely specified as the kingdom of Rome against the kingdom of God. That term "kingdom," by the way, emphasizes not so much territorial space, regional place, or ethnic identity as a mode of economic distribution, a type of human organization, and a style of world order, social justice, and global peace. That tectonic clash of kingdoms is the context of our Christmas texts.

What is fascinating is that the kingdom of Rome and the kingdom of God were each announced as the fifth and climactic kingdom of earth around the middle of that second century BCE. What is even more fascinating is the radically different content of each kingdom within that claim of an encompassing fifth and final age's program for the world.

That tectonic clash of the kingdom of Rome versus the kingdom of God—with each kingdom claiming to be the earth's fifth and final one—is the context for those Christmas stories in Matthew and Luke. They move, of course, within the kingdom of God over against the kingdom of Rome.

THE IMPERIAL KINGDOM OF ROME

Rome inherited from Greece the idea that world history would involve five great ages or kingdoms. The fifth kingdom would be, in other words, the last climactic kingdom of the whole world.

Soon after 30 CE, Caius Velleius Paterculus, legionary general and imperial administrator, wrote a two-volume *Compendium of Roman History* starting with the fall of Troy and ending around the year 29 CE. As he begins his account of how the gods "exalted this great empire of Rome to the highest point yet reached on earth" to become "the empire of the world" (2.131), he gives us this quotation:

> Aemilius Sura says in his book on the chronology of Rome: "The Assyrians were the first of all races to hold world power, then the Medes, and after them the Persians, and then the Macedonians. Then through the defeat of Kings Philip and Antiochus, of Macedonian origin, followed closely upon the overthrow of Carthage, the world power passed to the Roman people." (1.6)

Aemilius Sura, otherwise unknown, penned that serene assertion of Rome's global imperialism sometime after 146 BCE. The first four kingdoms of world history had already come and gone, and now Rome was the fifth, final, and climactic kingdom of earth. There was, in other words, a certain inevitability, a certain manifest destiny in all of this.

As we read those writers today, mockery comes all too easily. On the one hand, the smashed statues, broken walls, and shattered ruins of the Roman Empire litter the Mediterranean world, and storks build their nests on columns that once supported temple roofs. On the other, when Aemilius Sura wrote that triumphant declaration, the Roman Empire had a half millennium of destiny in the West yet remaining and, even after its collapse there, a full millennium in the East.

What, then, was the Roman Empire like the first century CE, when those Christian stories announced the miraculous birth of a divine child as the advent of the kingdom of God over against that kingdom of Rome? What was the Roman Empire like when Matthew announced that Jesus was the newborn Davidic Messiah and that, in him, God had appointed a new "King of the Jews" instead of that Rome-appointed Herod the Great (2:2)? And what was the Roman Empire like when Luke rejoiced that Jesus was the newborn Son of God and that, in him, God had "shown strength with his arm . . . scattered the proud in the thoughts of their hearts . . . brought down the powerful from their thrones, and lifted up the lowly . . . filled the hungry with good things, and sent the rich away empty" (1:51–53)?

Rome had established a very successful method for avoiding royal tyranny. Let there be no more kings, it said, but two aristocratic consuls chosen to govern together and only for one year. That system was powerful enough to defeat the troops and war elephants—more terrifying than tactical—of Hannibal and Carthage. But then something went terribly, terribly wrong. Athens had invented a democracy, but learned that you could have a democracy or an empire, but not both at the same time for long. Rome was now about to relearn that lesson. It had invented a republic, but was now to learn that you could have a republic or an empire, but not both at the same time for long.

One consul went west to conquer and loot Gaul. The other went east to conquer and loot Syria. And why thereafter should they cooperate or abdicate their power? As consuls became warlords, Rome was locked in its worst nightmare, civil war with battle-hardened legions on both sides. Rome had avoided tyranny only to obtain anarchy. First, Julius Caesar against Pompey; next, Caesar's adherents against Caesar's assassins; and, finally, Octavian, backed by Italy, against Mark Antony, backed by Egypt. After twenty years of civil war, it looked as if the Roman Empire was destroying itself and ruining much of the Mediterranean world in the process of its own destruction.

Then, on a calm Mediterranean day, September 2, 31 BCE, it all ended out in the Ionian Sea off Cape Actium in northwestern Greece. It was the last great naval battle of antiquity, and never had so much been gained for so many by so little. With their forces sapped by a summer of disease, desertion, and despair, Antony and Cleopatra fled to double suicide at Alexandria, leaving their troops to survive and surrender as best they could.

The victorious Octavian, grandnephew and adopted son of the deified Julius Caesar, would soon be entitled in Latin *Augustus,* the "One Who Is Divine," or in Greek *Sebastos,* the "One Who Is to Be Worshiped" (from *sebomai,* "to worship"). At Priene, just off the mid-Aegean coast of Turkey, for example, a temple's fallen lintel records its Greek dedication to THE AUTOCRAT CAESAR, THE SON OF GOD, THE GOD SEBASTOS.

The civil wars were over, and Rome had died as an imperial republic only to reinvent itself as an imperial monarchy.

And it held that imperial power strongly, firmly, and lengthily over very many centuries. But how?

We know from historical sociology that imperial power is something like a giant hawser holding the empire-as-ship to the earth-as-dock. And that hawser has four separate but interwoven strands of power—military, economic, political, and ideological power. It was not any one alone, but the full integration of those four types of power that constituted Roman strength. In what follows we spend the most space on Rome's ideological power, because those who celebrated the birth of Jesus in Matthew and Luke lacked any vestige of military, economic, or political power. They came with ideology against ideology or, more accurately, with theology against theology, so our emphasis here is on Roman imperial theology.

Military power is the monopoly or control of force and violence. That was based, of course, on the legions and, at the time of Jesus's birth, Rome had twenty-eight of them, each composed of five to six thousand fighting engineers. Their first job was conquest, but that included building an infrastructure on which their control depended—so all-weather ports, roads, and bridges came first. When the historian Josephus itemized a legionary's pack in his *Jewish War,* he cited only two items for war, but seven for construction.

Economic power is the monopoly or control of labor and production. Once that all-weather military infrastructure was in place, it could also be used for trade and commerce. Furthermore, the legions were not centralized as a strategic reserve near Rome, but stretched along the frontiers and paid there in cash. So the contact zones of the frontier were slowly but steadily monetized and eventually planted with veterans. That has been correctly described as a legionary economy.

Afterward, and very soon, came cities, temples, and statues, aqueducts, baths, and amphitheaters.

Political power is the monopoly or control of organization and institution. Think about this absurdity. In the waning years of the nineteenth century, at the height of the British Empire, a Tory Member of Parliament declares that a brilliant Indian barrister would make a great prime minister of England. Why absurd? Racism, of course. But for Rome the equivalent was utterly possible. Once a "barbarian" province was properly Romanized, some of its higher aristocrats could become members of the Senate, and one of them could even become emperor.

Ideological power is the monopoly or control of meaning and interpretation. We begin by looking ahead. The titles of the Roman emperor Caesar Augustus were: Divine, Son of God, God, God from God, Lord, Redeemer, Liberator, and Savior of the World. To use any of them of the newborn Jesus would be either low lampoon or high treason. And, since empires always know their opponents, Rome was not laughing. But for now, what did those titles mean as applied to Caesar Augustus? Without knowing that we will never understand what they meant when transferred by some Jews to Jesus.

The Greco-Roman tradition knew of immortal gods and goddesses (a *deus* or a *dea*) who controlled the world—although in some competition with one another. But it also recognized humans who became divine (a *divus* or a *diva*), individuals who were deified, but only for extraordinary or transcendental service to the world. As the Augustan poet Horace noted in his *Epistles,* that normally happened after their death, but "upon you [Augustus], however, while still living among us, we already bestow divine honors, set up altars to swear by in your name, and confess that nobody like you will arise hereafter or has ever arisen before now" (2.1). The human Augustus was divinity incarnate.

If you look back to that long afternoon off Cape Actium, you can see what Horace meant. After almost a hundred years of social unrest and twenty years of interminable civil war, Octavian, the Augustus-to-be, had saved the Roman Empire and brought peace to the Mediterranean. Imagine a great simultaneous sigh of sincere relief around that Roman lake, a thanks be to God, as it were, but since Octavian had done it, was he not God? Was he not Savior of the World? And that almost instant upgrade from Son of God—son, that is, of the already divine Julius Caesar—to God in his own right was not just because of Augustus's personality or even character, but because of his program. What, then, was Augustus's proclaimed program for the new and improved Roman Empire? You can see it clearly announced after Actium.

Immediately after that battle and even before pursuing his fleeing enemies to Alexandria, Octavian ordered a new Victory City, a Nicopolis, to be created in commemoration of his triumph. No surprise there. But also, in a striking equation of his own and Rome's destiny, he turned his camp into sacred ground and ordered a memorial atop the tent site from which he went forth to battle that September morning. Along the open front of its three-sided portico, he placed a tithe of the three hundred or so bronze attack rams from the prows of the defeated fleet. And above it he inscribed in tall Latin letters—many still extant on site—the dedication that summarized for him the heart of Roman imperial theology. He offered religious thanks to the war god, Mars, and the sea god, Neptune, for the war he had fought, for the victory he had obtained, and for the peace that had ensued.

And there you have the four successive elements of Roman imperial theology—*religion, war, victory, peace*. You worship the gods, you go to war with their assistance, you are victorious with their help, and you obtain peace from their generosity. And the key phrase from that monument is: "Victory [with] peace secured on land and sea." For Augustus and for Rome it was always about peace, but always about peace through victory, peace through war, peace through violence.

It is vital to understand Augustus's program of *peace through victory,* because it is presumed in the counterprogram of those Christmas stories and by the gospels to which they are the parabolic overtures. But is there any other program for earth besides *peace through victory*? We move now to answer that question and to consider an alternative vision for peace on earth.

THE ESCHATOLOGICAL KINGDOM OF GOD

The adjective *eschatological* (from the Greek *eschata,* or "last things") is a term in biblical scholarship referring to God's vision for that fifth or final kingdom of earth, for how the world would be run if God were its direct ruler (we might ask what a divine budget would look like). The *eschaton* denotes earth's last and final kingdom, or, in other words, the kingdom of God.

Eschatology is not, of course, about the destruction of the earth, but about its transfiguration, not about the end of the world, but about the end of evil, injustice, violence—and imperialism. Think of the *eschaton* as the Great Divine Cleanup of the World. And to consider this eschatological kingdom of God we begin, as with the imperial kingdom of Rome above, in the middle of the second century BCE.

Earlier in that century the situation in tiny Israel was even more than usually dangerous. The Greco-Syrian monarch Antiochus IV Epiphanes ruled one of the three major segments of Alexander's vast empire, which had once stretched from the plains of Macedonia to the mountains of India. But, by the early 160s BCE, in an attempt to integrate Israel fully into his realm and to eliminate any faith-based opposition to that program, he launched a religious persecution against Judaism itself. Some Jews responded with very successful military resistance, and you can read their story in 1 Maccabees (a book in the Roman Catholic but not the Protestant version of the Christian Bible). But other Jews thought that the fundamental problem was not about Israel and Syria, but about God and empire, and you can read about their response in the book of Daniel (a book in both those canons).

The author of the latter book created an imaginary Jewish seer named Daniel living in a fictional Mesopotamian situation over three hundred years earlier than the factual Syrian situation of the early 160s BCE, when the book was actually written. We focus on one specific chapter in it.

Daniel 7 begins with a dream vision in which there is, once again, a sequence of four great empires—those of Babylonia, Medea, Persia, and Macedonia. But those imperial powers are described not as human forces arising from the orderly land, but as feral animals arising from the disorderly ocean: "I, Daniel, saw in my vision by night the four winds of heaven stirring up the great sea, and four great beasts came up out of the sea, different from one another," and "these four great beasts [are] four kings [that] shall arise out of the earth" (7:2–3, 17). These are Daniel's four empires:

1. *Babylonian Empire:* "The first was like a lion and had eagles' wings." (7:4)

2. *Medean Empire:* "Another beast appeared, a second one, that looked like a bear." (7:5)

3. *Persian Empire:* "After this, as I watched, another appeared, like a leopard." (7:6)

4. *Macedonian Empire:* "After this I saw in the visions by night a fourth beast, terrifying and dreadful and exceedingly strong. It had great iron teeth and was devouring, breaking in pieces, and stamping what was left with its feet. It was different from all the beasts that preceded it." (7:7)

That fourth empire is more fearful than all those earlier ones put together, and no beast image could do it justice. Nothing had ever struck the East like the serried ranks of Macedonian pikes as Alexander invented annihilation rather than mere victory as the purpose of battle.

The Greco-Syrian empire of the 160s BCE is not even counted as another empire. It is but a subempire of Alexander's. It is only one of the horns of that Macedonian beast. It is, indeed, only "a little horn" (7:8). But then comes Daniel's vision of the fifth, final, and climactic empire of earth, the eschatological kingdom of God.

At a great trial held in heaven, God condemned all those past empires including that Syrian subempire. In the trial, "the court sat in judgment, and the books were opened." At the judgment, "their dominion was taken away" (7:10–12). All empires, and with them imperialism itself, are condemned by divine judgment. But what replaced them as the fifth and final kingdom or empire of earth? Each of those four empires was symbolized as a single beast from the depths. The fifth and final kingdom is also symbolized, but as a human being from the heights. As they were "like" eagle, bear, leopard, and some ultra-animal, it is "like a son of man," that is, "like a human being." (In English "humankind" often appears chauvinistically as "mankind." Similarly, in Semitic languages "human being" often appears chauvinistically as "man" or "son of man.") What is at stake in Daniel is this: the first four empires are inhuman beasts; only the fifth and final empire is truly human.

The vision of the world's climactic kingdom is given twice, first to that symbolic humanlike one and thence to all those incorporated within that personification. It must be emphasized that just as those individual beastlike ones represent and contain an entire community, so also here, the individual humanlike one represents and contains an entire community. "To him" means "to the people of the holy ones of the Most High":

"To him was given dominion and glory and kingship, that all peoples, nations, and languages should serve him. His dominion is an everlasting dominion that shall not pass away, and his kingship is one that shall never be destroyed." (7:14)	"The kingship and dominion and the greatness of the kingdoms under the whole heaven shall be given to the people of the holy ones of the Most High; their kingdom shall be an everlasting kingdom, and all dominions shall serve and obey them." (7:27)

You will notice two aspects of that climax. The fifth and final kingdom, the kingdom of God, is here a glorious future option—it is given in heaven to "one like a human being" (literally: "one like a son of man") to be brought down to earth for all. But neither is Daniel's final kingdom specified in any great detail.

So there is still this question: how exactly is the alleged final and eschatological kingdom of God different from the final and imperial kingdom of Rome? Each claimed to be divinely decreed, eternally mandated, and transcendentally guaranteed. Each claimed to be universal and everlasting, to be unlimited across time and space. What then was the difference between them?

To pursue that crucial question we come down a century and a half to look at a Jewish text from the age of Augustus, a text contemporary with the birth of Jesus. Here you can see most clearly how God's eschatological kingdom differs from all those imperial empires—including Rome itself. The text is from one of the Jewish *Sibylline Oracles,* a series of fictional prophecies that Judaism and then Christianity borrowed from Rome and then used rather fiercely against that very tradition:

> The earth will belong equally to all, undivided by walls or fences. It will then bear more abundant fruits spontaneously. Lives will be in common and wealth will have no division. For there will be no poor man there, no rich, and no tyrant, no slave. Further, no one will be either great or small anymore. No kings, no leaders. All will be on a par together. (2.319–24)

For that ultimate vision, by the way, the model was not democracy, but family. God is like the Father who must provide equally for all the family of the earth—equally, meaning enough for everyone always.

We can now see that the fundamental difference between those divergent visions of earth's final kingdom is not about ends, but about means. The imperial kingdom of Rome—and this may indeed apply to any other empire as well—had as its program *peace through victory*. The eschatological kingdom of God has as its program *peace through justice*. Both intend peace—one by violence, the other by nonviolence. And still those tectonic plates grind against one another.

Finally, two major questions arise from that vision of God's eschatological kingdom, of God's Great Cleanup of the World, of God's visionary program of peace through justice. First, what would God do to the Gentiles, the non-Jews, on that great day of transformation? Second, would God use some mediator or manager, some vicar or viceroy, to establish that transformation?

THE FATE OF THE GENTILES

First, then, what about the Gentiles? This is not an indication of Jewish chauvinism or xenophobia. The Gentiles were the *gentes,* the nations, and those that homeland Jews knew best and intended most were the great empires that had always oppressed them. So this was the question. When the great day for the earth's divine transformation arrived, what would God do with the current great empire of that time? If it happened in the first century, for instance, what would God do with the Romans? The Bible—both the preceding Jewish scriptures and the later Christian scriptures—gave two diametrically opposed answers to this very basic question.

One answer was extermination in a *Great Final Battle* at the symbolic place of Mt. Megiddo—the Hebrew term is Har Megiddo, whence our English term "Armageddon" in that last book of the Christine Bible, the Apocalypse or Revelation. According to Micah, God would simply destroy the current great empire:

> In anger and wrath I will execute vengeance on the nations that did not obey.... Then my enemy will see, and

shame will cover her who said to me, "Where is the Lord your God?" My eyes will see her downfall; now she will be trodden down like the mire of the streets. . . . The nations shall see and be ashamed of all their might; they shall lay their hands on their mouths; their ears shall be deaf; they shall lick dust like a snake, like the crawling things of the earth; they shall come trembling out of their fortresses; they shall turn in dread to the Lord our God, and they shall stand in fear of you. (Mic. 5:15; 7:10, 16–17)

And that is quite mild compared to the later Christian program for that Great Final Battle in the book of Revelation, where "the wine press was trodden outside the city, and blood flowed from the wine press, as high as a horse's bridle, for a distance of about two hundred miles" (14:20).

Another answer was conversion in a *Great Final Feast* at the symbolic place of Mt. Zion. All the nations would be converted, not to Judaism, but to the God of justice and peace. Here is that magnificent vision. It is also from Micah, but is repeated verbatim—except for the final verse—in Isaiah 2:2–4:

In days to come the mountain of the Lord's house shall be established as the highest of the mountains, and shall be raised up above the hills. Peoples shall stream to it, and many nations shall come and say: "Come, let us go up to the mountain of the Lord, to the house of the God of Jacob; that he may teach us his ways and that we may walk in his paths." For out of Zion shall go forth instruction, and the word of the Lord from Jerusalem. He shall judge between many peoples, and shall arbitrate between strong nations far away; they shall beat their swords into plowshares, and their spears into pruning hooks; nation shall not lift up sword against nation, neither shall they learn war any more; but they shall all sit under their own vines and under their own fig trees, and no one shall make them afraid; for the mouth of the Lord of hosts has spoken. (Mic. 4:1–3)

Along with that vision of a great divine arbitration among all the nations to establish war no more, there will also be a great feast with the very best food and drink:

On this mountain the Lord of hosts will make for all peoples a feast of rich food, a feast of well-aged wines, of rich food filled with marrow, of well-aged wines strained clear. And he will destroy on this mountain the shroud that is cast over all peoples, the sheet that is spread over all nations; he will swallow up death forever. Then the Lord God will wipe away the tears from all faces, and the disgrace of his people he will take away from all the earth, for the Lord has spoken. (Isa. 25:6–8)

There are, in other words, two utterly divergent descriptions of God's final solution to the existence of imperialism, one violent and the other nonviolent, one extermination in a Great Final Battle and the other conversion at a Great Final Feast. They are both there from one end of the Christian Bible to the other. Which one, do you think, is announced by those Christmas stories? When Luke's angels announce "peace on earth" to those shepherds at Bethlehem, is it peace through victory or peace through justice?

The Advent of the Messiah

Next comes the second of those two questions given above. Comes that day of the Great Divine Cleanup of the World, would God use some intermediary figure for that transformation of the world? Would God have some Messiah or Christ— that is, some Anointed One—as viceroy or administrator for the establishment on earth of the kingdom of God?

Here are two examples of that pre-Christian Jewish expectation of such a Messiah. They are deliberately chosen because one speaks of that eschatological viceroy as "Son of David" and "Lord Messiah," while the other lacks those titles but speaks instead of "Son of God" and "Son of the Most High." They both date to the final half of the first century BCE.

The first example is from the *Psalms of Solomon*. Its matrix is the first direct experience of violent Roman power within the Jewish homeland. Pompey conquered Jerusalem and desecrated its temple in 63 BCE: "A man alien to our race ... a lawless one laid waste our land. . . . He did in Jerusalem all the things that gentiles do for their gods in their cities" (17:7, 11, 14). But in 48 BCE Pompey was assassinated on an Egyptian beach: "His body was carried about on the waves in much shame, and there was no one to bury him" (2:27). So surely soon, surely now, God would,

> raise up for them their king, the Son of David ... to smash the arrogance of sinners like a potter's jar; to shatter all their substance with an iron rod; to destroy the unlawful nations with the word of his mouth. . . . He will judge peoples and nations in the wisdom of his righteousness. . . . All shall be holy, and their king shall be the Lord Messiah. (For) he will not rely on horse and rider

and bow, nor will he collect gold and silver for war. Nor will he build up hope in a multitude for a day of war. (17:21, 23–24, 29, 32–33)

On the one hand, this coming Messiah is not exactly a pacifist, and the Romans seem destined for extermination rather than conversion—recall those two eschatological alternatives from above. On the other hand, he is certainly not a military Messiah organizing a rebellion against Rome. Notice that phrase about "the word of his mouth" (17:24) and its later repetition as "the word of his mouth" (17:35) and "the strength of his word" (17:36). That ability to destroy one's enemies by "word" alone is a transcendental ability akin to the creative word of God in Genesis 1.

The other example is from a Dead Sea Scroll fragment found in Cave 4 at Qumran—hence its designation 4Q246:

He will be called Son of God, and they will call him Son of the Most High. Like sparks of a vision, so will their kingdom be; they will rule several years over the earth and crush everything; a people will crush another people, and a city another city. Until the people of God arises [or: until he raises up the people of God] and makes everyone rest from the sword. His kingdom will be an eternal kingdom, and all his paths in truth and uprightness. The earth will be in truth and all will make peace. The sword will cease in the earth, and all the cities will pay him homage. He is a great god among the gods [or: The great God will be his strength]. He will make war with him; he will place the peoples in his hand and cast away everyone before him. His kingdom will be an eternal kingdom . . .

You can see in that text, as with the "one like a human being" in Daniel 7 above, that an individual figure, "Son of God" or "Son of the Most High," has an "eternal kingdom" along with "the people of God."

Those two texts serve to emphasize two very complex questions concerning the expectation of an intermediary protagonist for God's eschatological transformation of the world. First, is this figure to be violent or nonviolent? And, if violent, how will that violence operate? Second, is this figure to be human or transcendent? And, if transcendent, how will that transcendence operate?

One final point. It is not accurate to distinguish the imperial kingdom of Rome from the eschatological kingdom of God by claiming one is earthly the other heavenly, one is evil the other holy, or one is demonic the other sublime. That is simply name-calling. Both come to us with divine credentials for the good of humanity. They are two alternative transcendental visions. *Empire* promises peace through violent force. *Eschaton* promises peace through nonviolent justice. Each requires programs and processes, strategies and tactics, wisdom and patience. If you consider that peace through victory has been a highly successful vision across recorded history, why would you abandon it now? But whether you think it has been successful or not, you should at least know there has always been present an alternative option—peace through justice.

That clash of visionary programs for our earth is the context and matrix for those Christmas stories, and they proclaim God's peace through justice over against Rome's peace through victory. But before we turn to consider them in detail in this book's Part II, we look one more time at the Roman Empire in the Jewish homeland around the time Jesus was born.

The View from the Nazareth Ridge

In scholarship's best reconstruction, Jesus was born just before the death of Herod the Great in 4 BCE. But upon that death, there were uprisings all over the Jewish homeland, and some of them had clearly messianic overtones—violent attempts to replace an unjust and Rome-appointed tyrant with a just and God-appointed ruler. But at that time there were no first-rank legionary forces, only second-rank auxiliary troops stationed in Israel. So, in order to put down those rebellions, the Syrian legions guarding the Euphrates frontier against the Parthian Empire—Rome's only serious threat—had to strip that protective screen and leave their northern bases. They came, in other words, not only to fight, but to punish as well. When we are finished with you this time, they said, we will not have to return at least for a couple of generations. There was, among those rebellions, one at Sepphoris, capital of the Galilee, just a few miles north of Nazareth. There, according to Josephus's *Jewish War,* a rebel named Judas "raised a considerable body of followers, broke open the royal arsenals, and, having armed his companions, attacked the other aspirants to power" (2.56).

Rome had three legions in Syria; the governor, Varus, sent first one and then two more of them southward to Israel. That meant, as you will recall from above, about eighteen thousand elite troops accompanied by two thousand auxiliary cavalry and fifteen hundred auxiliary infantry. Their staging area was at Ptolemais on the Mediterranean coast due west of Sepphoris. Then, as Varus took his main force south, he "at once sent a detachment of his army into the region of Galilee adjoining Ptolemais, under the command of his friend Gaius; the latter routed all who opposed him, captured and burnt the city of Sepphoris and reduced its inhabitants to slavery" (2.68).

What do you think happened to small adjacent villages when the legions struck their local city with fire and sword? What do you think happened to Nazareth, a tiny hamlet about four miles, or an hour and a half's walk, over the Nazareth ridge and across the floor of the Beth Netopha valley?

Josephus does not give any detailed description of what happened around Sepphoris in 4 BCE, but we can apply to Nazareth what happened when the Syrian legions under Vespasian marched southward against the next rebellion in 67–68 CE. At Gerasa, or Jerash, on the other side of the Jordan from Sepphoris, Lucius Annius "put to the sword a thousand of the youth, who had not already escaped, made prisoners of women and children, gave his soldiers license to plunder the property, and then set fire to the houses and advanced against the surrounding villages. The able-bodied fled, the feeble perished, and everything left was consigned to the flames" (4.488–89).

For Nazareth, in 4 BCE, either there was timely flight to hiding places well known to the local peasantry, or its males were murdered, its females raped, and its children enslaved. If they escaped, the little they had would be gone when they returned because, as another rebel said, when you had nothing, the Romans took even that. "They make a desert and call it peace."

Jesus grew up in Nazareth after 4 BCE, so this is our claim. The major event in his village's life was *the day the Romans came*. As he grew up toward Luke's coming-of-age at twelve, he could not *not* have heard, again and again and again, about *the day of the Romans*—who had escaped and who had not, who had lived and who had died. The Romans were not some distant mythological beings; they were soldiers who had devastated Nazareth's backyard around the time of his birth. So this is how we *imagine,* as close to history as possible, what his actual coming-of-age might have entailed.

One day, when he was old enough, Mary took Jesus up to the top of the Nazareth ridge. It was springtime, the breeze had cleared the air, and the wildflowers were already everywhere. Across the valley, Sepphoris gleamed white on its green hill. "We knew they were coming," Mary said, "but your father had not come home. So we waited after the others were gone. Then we heard the noise, and the earth trembled a little. We did too, but your father had still not come home. Finally, we saw the dust and we had to flee, but your father never came home. I brought you up here today so you will always remember that day we lost him and what little else we had. We lived, yes, but with these questions. Why did God not defend those who defended God? Where was God that day the Romans came?"

PART II

GENEALOGY, CONCEPTION, AND BIRTH

CHAPTER FOUR

GENEALOGY AS DESTINY

Most Christians and many non-Christians could tell you the basic story of the conception and birth of Jesus. But they would probably never mention the detailed genealogies given to him in Matthew 1:1–17 and Luke 3:23–38. That may well be wise, because to start with a long list of ancestors may be the best way to kill a story—see Appendix 1. We ourselves are aware of that risk in starting here with those genealogical lists. We do so quite deliberately, because they are a first and most emphatic signal about the nature and purpose of these two nativity stories. Nowhere is it so clear as in these two genealogies that theological metaphor and symbolic parable rather than actual history and factual information create and dominate the Christmas stories of the conception and infancy of Jesus.

We are willing to make that point in even stronger terms. If you understand properly what minimal history but maximal theology those genealogies contain, you will recognize the similar balance in the Christmas stories as a whole. Understand the purpose of these genealogies, and you will understand the purpose of the parabolic overtures in Matthew and Luke. In fact, just as the overtures are miniatures of the gospels, so are the genealogies miniatures of the overtures.

Here is the sequence for this chapter. First, we look at the differences and then the similarities between those two genealogies. Next, based on that data, we interpret the separate function of each genealogy—first Matthew's, then Luke's—in terms of their specific Christmas stories and succeeding gospels. Finally, returning to that first-century historical context, we ask why genealogies were significant enough for both evangelists to create them quite independently from one another—and quite differently from one another.

Different Genealogies for the Same Jesus

We begin with the differences between the genealogies of Jesus in Matthew 1:1–17 and Luke 3:23–38 (you can see their full texts in Appendix 1). The point of emphasizing these differences is not to underline their biographical mistakes or criticize their historical discrepancies, but to understand their religious functions and accept their theological intentions.

Location. The most striking difference is that Matthew's genealogy comes at the very start of his Christmas story, while Luke's genealogy comes at the start of Jesus's public life—after his baptism, in fact—and therefore outside his Christmas story.

Direction. There are two rather obvious ways of presenting a genealogical list. One is to list the names down from parents to children, ancestors to descendants. The other is to list them up from children to parents, descendants to ancestors.

Matthew's genealogy follows that former pattern, and Luke's the latter:

	Abraham		Jesus
Matthew's Genealogy:	↓	*Luke's Genealogy:*	↓
	Jesus		Adam

That choice of direction—forward from Abraham for Matthew or backward to Adam for Luke—does not seem to be based on any significant reason. They are just the two obvious options.

Format. Neither do the differences in style have any significant purpose. Matthew says, for example, that "Abraham was the father of Isaac" (1:2), and so on, in the New Revised Standard Version's way of rephrasing the King James Version's famous "Abraham begat Isaac," and so on. Luke's method is even briefer: "Isaac [son] of Abraham" (3:34), so that, in Greek, we have a simple series of names, one after another, in the genitive case.

Number. Matthew speaks of 14 + 14 + 14, or 42, "generations" from Abraham to Jesus, but that count seems impossible to sustain in any literal sense, as you can see in Appendix 1. If you check it in terms of generations by counting every "*x* was the father of *y*," you obtain 13 + 14 + 13, or 40 generations. And if you focus on individuals by counting every *x* and *y*, but each one only once, you get 14 + 14 + 13 names, or 41 individuals. It is wiser, with either count, to presume theological rather than mathematical purpose behind Matthew's balanced claim of a 14 + 14 + 14 rhythm. But we have more on this below. Luke, on the other hand, has no numerical discrepancies, since he simply presents 77 generations—possibly as 7 × 11?—but never offers any count for either individuals or generations on his list, as you can see in Appendix 1.

Discrepancy. Even where Matthew and Luke give the same names between Abraham and Jesus, they go their very separate ways (see Appendix 1). They agree on the six names from Abraham to Hezron, on the seven names from Aminadab to David, and on the two names Salathiel/Shealtiel and Zerubbabel. But here are two rather striking differences. One is that Matthew's list descends from David through Solomon (a king), but Luke's descends from David through Nathan (a prophet). The other is that Matthew names Jesus's grandfather as Jacob, but Luke names him as Heli. Any attempt at reconciling those versions for historical accuracy is love's labor lost. They are parabolic lists, not historical records, and we return below to consider their separate purposes.

Granted those many differences, are there any significant agreements between those two genealogies?

Structure. Both genealogies signal their emphasis with very specific sentences at the beginning and end of their lists:

Matthew's Genealogy	*Luke's Genealogy*
"An account of the genealogy of Jesus the Messiah, the son of David, the son of Abraham." (1:1)	"Jesus was the son (as was thought) of Joseph." (3:23)
↓	↓
Multiple individuals and generations (1:2–16)	Multiple individuals and generations (3:24–37)
↓	↓
"So all the generations from Abraham to David are fourteen generations; and from David to the deportation to Babylon, fourteen generations; and from the deportation to Babylon to the Messiah, fourteen generations." (1:17)	"son of Adam, son of God" (3:38)

Patriarchy. The most striking agreement between the two genealogies is their male emphasis or patriarchal bias. Although they both claim that Jesus's conception involved *a female generating a son without a male,* you would almost imagine that all those other generations consisted of *males generating sons without females* — except, of course, for the four exceptions, Tamar in Matthew 1:3, Rahab and Ruth in 1:5, and the unnamed "wife of Uriah" in 1:6.

Fathers beget sons in Matthew and sons have fathers in Luke, but mothers are strangely absent in both—except again for those four Matthean exceptions. Even Mary herself is not mentioned in the genealogy of Luke 3:23, although she is in that of Matthew 1:16. Where have all the mothers gone?

We consider below why Matthew mentioned those four specific mothers despite his general format of fathers begetting sons with mothers unmentioned, but for now we look briefly at one ancient contemporary Jewish context where that same patriarchal bias seems equally evident.

In the 90s CE, the Jewish historian Flavius Josephus describes his own precocious coming-of-age wisdom in his autobiographical *Life* (see our Appendix 3). And he prefaces that story with his genealogy. He claims that his "family is no ignoble one, tracing its descent far back to priestly ancestors" and that "with us a connection with the priesthood is the hallmark of an illustrious line" (1).

Josephus continues with this second claim: "Moreover, on my mother's side I am of royal blood" (1.2b). He then describes his maternal connection to the Hasmonean, or Maccabean, dynasty of priest-kings who ruled Israel for a hundred years before the Romans arrived around the middle of the first century BCE and replaced them with the Herodians. He gives his royal genealogy going back five generations to his "great-grandfather's grandfather" around 135 BCE (3–5):

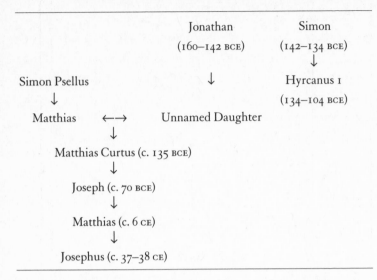

When you examine that short genealogy, certain elements jump out immediately. Josephus works forward from Simon to himself—from past to present, as Matthew does for Jesus—rather than backward from himself to Simon—from present to past, as Luke does for Jesus. And all the names are male. Even though he emphasizes his royal connections, he never names that female princess—she is simply "the daughter of Jonathan the high priest." Nine male names are mentioned in that genealogy, but not a single female name appears there—not even that most important princess from whom alone Josephus could claim royal descent. This is surely patriarchal bias, which appears as well in both Matthew's and Luke's genealogies.

Finally, notice that Josephus claims ancestry from both the priestly and royal rulers of his people. That combination is the highest Jewish pedigree for that time and place. Luke—but not Matthew—gives a similar double pedigree to Jesus. He is of priestly lineage through Mary and of royal lineage through

Joseph. Elizabeth "was a descendant of Aaron" (1:5) and Mary is her "relative" (1:36). Joseph "was descended from the house and family of David" (2:4).

The Genealogy of the Son of David

Matthew begins his version of the gospel in 1:1 as "an account of the genealogy of Jesus the Messiah, the son of David, the son of Abraham." That gives us his immediate purpose and the content of his genealogical proclamation. He ends in 1:17 with this: "So all the generations from Abraham to David are fourteen generations; and from David to the deportation to Babylon, fourteen generations; and from the deportation to Babylon to the Messiah, fourteen generations." In other words, Matthew has structured Jesus's ancestry in three time segments:

1. Abraham to David (c. 750 years): 13 generations with 14 individual male names and 3 female names

2. David to the Babylonian exile (c. 400 years): 14 generations with 14 new individual male names and 1 female designation

3. The Babylonian exile to Jesus's birth (c. 575 years): 13 generations with 13 new male names and 1 female name

Even within his own names and protocols, it is not at all clear how Matthew computes those 14 generations. But, apart from his mathematical inaccuracy, his theological point is very clear. If there were around 14 generations from Abraham to David, and then 14 more from David to the Babylonian exile, one would expect something of equally transcendental importance to happen after about another 14 generations. Clearly, some divine patterning was established to indicate the appropriate time for the birth of Jesus. We are dealing, in other words, with parabolic mathematics.

You will also notice that, even though both Matthew and Luke give wildly divergent genealogies of Joseph—even with different fathers for Joseph—they both guard against letting anyone think that he is the biological father of Jesus. As you will recall, Luke 3:23 begins with Jesus, "the son (as was thought) of Joseph son of Heli." The corresponding line in Matthew speaks of "Jacob the father of Joseph the husband of Mary, of whom Jesus was born, who is called the Messiah" (1:16). In Greek, that "of whom" is feminine and refers to Mary, not Joseph.

As you will have noticed, Matthew begins in 1:1 and ends in 1:18 with Jesus as the "Messiah." Matthew 1:1–18 gives us the genealogy of Jesus as the "Messiah," just as Luke 3:23b–38 gives us the genealogy of Jesus as the "Son of God." But there is still one very special feature of Matthew. There were no female names given for Josephus's genealogy in his *Life,* although there was one female designation—"the daughter of Jonathan the high priest." There are neither female names nor designations in Jesus's Lukan genealogy—even after all his emphasis on Mary. But Jesus's genealogy in Matthew contains four female names and one female designation, given here literally from the Greek and italicized to emphasize their connections:

"Judah *begot* Perez and Zerah *from* Tamar" (1:3)

"Salmon *begot* Boaz *from* Rahab" (1:5a)

"Boaz *begot* Obed *from* Ruth" (1:5b)

"David *begot* Solomon *from* the [wife] of Uriah" (1:6)

"Joseph the husband of Mary, *from* whom Jesus was
begotten" (1:16)

The passive voice in Mary's begetting of Jesus means "begotten by God." Since there were obviously unnamed females involved in every single one of those three sets of 14 generations,
the first four designated females must have special purpose for
Matthew especially in connection with Mary. But what exactly
is it and who are those first four women?

Tamar. Er and Onan were the sons of the Israelite Judah
and the Canaanite Shua in Genesis 38. Er married a Canaanite woman named Tamar and, when he was later struck dead
by God, his brother Onan should have married Tamar to create children in the dead Er's name. (That procedure was commanded in Deuteronomy 25:5–10 most likely to prevent the
alienation of family property, and you may recall it from the
question put to Jesus in Mark 12:18–27.) But instead, Onan
"spilled his semen on the ground" (38:9) and was also struck
dead by God. Judah defaulted on marrying his third son,
Shelah, to Tamar, so she took matters into her own hands. She
covered her face, Judah thought her a prostitute, and bore him
twin sons, whom he had to acknowledge: " 'She is more in the
right than I, since I did not give her to my son Shelah.' And he
did not lie with her again" (38:26).

Rahab. At the end of the exodus from Egypt, Joshua sent
Israelite spies ahead to reconnoiter "the land" (Josh. 2). Rahab
was a Canaanite prostitute from Jericho. She hid the spies from
the city's authorities, lied about their whereabouts, and finally
"let them down by a rope through the window, for her house
was on the outer side of the city wall and she resided within
the wall itself " (2:15). In return, Rahab asked for protection

when the Israelites came to attack Jericho; the spies promised her future safety and eventually gave it to her and her family (6:22–23).

Ruth. An Israelite couple, Naomi and Elimelech, left their home at Bethlehem and went to Moab in the book of Ruth. They had two sons, Mahlon and Chilion, who married Moabite wives, Orpah and Ruth. All three men died, and Naomi decided to immigrate to Israel, telling her daughters-in-law to stay in Moab and get new husbands for themselves. But Ruth refused to leave Naomi, saying, in these justly famous lines: " 'Do not press me to leave you or to turn back from following you! Where you go, I will go; where you lodge, I will lodge; your people shall be my people, and your God my God. Where you die, I will die—there will I be buried. May the Lord do thus and so to me, and more as well, if even death parts me from you!' " (1:16–17).

They arrive at Bethlehem to live among Naomi's kinfolk. In a delicately described scene, Ruth, instructed by Naomi, seduces Boaz (3:1–15). Then, since Elimelech's nearest kinsman will not marry her, Boaz agrees to do so—you will recall that kinship obligation from the similar case of Tamar above. Their firstborn son is "Obed; he became the father of Jesse, the father of David. Now these are the descendants of Perez: Perez begot Hezron, Hezron begot Ram, Ram begot Amminadab, Amminadab begot Nahshon, Nahshon begot Salmon, Salmon begot Boaz, Boaz begot Obed, Obed begot Jesse, and Jesse begot David" (4:17–22, literal translation).

You can see the resemblance in style between David's genealogical format there and Jesus's genealogy in Matthew. It descends forward in strictly male lineage from father to son, and each "begetting" lacks mention of the mother. Also, despite two minor differences, that sequence of nine genera-

tions and ten male names from Perez to David is taken up as
an agreement by Matthew 1:3–6 and Luke 3:31–33. Finally,
Ruth is repeatedly identified as "Ruth the Moabite," even
though Deuteronomy 23:3–4 explicitly states: "No Ammonite
or Moabite shall be admitted to the assembly of the Lord.
Even to the tenth generation, none of their descendants shall
be admitted to the assembly of the Lord, because they did not
meet you with food and water on your journey out of Egypt."
Still, despite all of that, Ruth, a Moabite woman, is the great-
grandmother of David.

Bathsheba. David committed adultery with Bathsheba, the wife
of a Hittite warrior, Uriah, who fought in his army (2 Sam. 11).
When she conceived, David brought Uriah back from the
front so that he might think his was the conception. When
that failed, David ordered Uriah placed "in the forefront of
the hardest fighting, . . . so that he may be struck down and
die" (11:15). Once Uriah had been killed in action, "David sent
and brought Bathsheba to his house, and she became his wife,
and bore him a son" (11:27). It died, and Solomon, with intervention from his mother, Bathsheba, and the prophet Nathan,
became king after David (1 Kings 1).

The question is not what resemblances we might imagine
between those four mothers and Mary, but what we think
Matthew intended to emphasize by mentioning all five in similar language.

A first answer is that the first four were all Gentiles—Rahab
and Ruth explicitly so, Tamar and Bathsheba presumably so.
You might object that that does not connect them to Mary,
since she was a Jewish and not a gentile woman. However,
since Matthew emphasizes the inclusion of Gentiles alongside

Jews in the infancy story—the Persian Magi, for example—he may have intended to symbolize that interaction by including gentile women in the genealogy of Jesus. And that must always remain a possibility.

A second answer has the advantage of connecting all five mothers together. In every case there was a marital abnormality, but it was precisely through those five somewhat surprising or irregular unions that God controlled the lineage of the Messiah. It has also been suggested that the women took the initiative and moved boldly to solve the irregularity. But, although that is certainly true for Tamar, Rahab, Ruth, and maybe even Bathsheba with regard to Solomon's royal ascendancy, it is hardly true for Mary—as Matthew, rather than Luke, narrates the infancy of Jesus. "It is," concludes Father Raymond Brown in his magisterial 1993 study *The Birth of the Messiah,* "the combination of the scandalous or irregular union and of divine intervention through the women that explains best Matthew's choice in the genealogy."[1]

We who live in a world that has discovered DNA think of maternity and paternity, descent and genealogy as matters of literal fact and historical actuality. We seldom think of a parabolic or symbolic genealogy and especially not one that includes specific name after specific name. We might stress a metaphorical descent, but usually without such details. For example, we might say of a too rich matriarch that she thinks her ancestors came over on the *Mayflower* or of a too proud president that he thinks he was born in a log cabin. In both those cases, we would immediately recognize that nothing literal was being said about ancestry on a ship or in a cabin. Those are simply sarcastic put-downs, metaphors against immodesty, and not claims on history.

In both its generalities and specifics, Matthew's genealogy of Jesus structures his destiny and defends his conception metaphorically and parabolically. That leaves us with another question for our next chapter. Why did Matthew find it necessary to defend Mary by linking her to those other ancestral women?

THE GENEALOGY OF THE SON OF GOD

As we saw above, the genealogies of Jesus could hardly be more divergent in Matthew and Luke. But the specific content and even the present position of each account is quite deliberately intentional for each author.

Unlike Matthew 1–2, Luke 1–2 does not begin the infancy story with a genealogy. Instead, Luke locates it not only after Jesus's coming-of-age story in 2:41–52, but after his account of John the Baptizer in 3:1–20—a full account of John from preaching to prison—and the baptism of Jesus in 3:20–23. Only then does he give Jesus's genealogy. But if you focus on that present gospel location and concentrate on the opening and closing verses of the genealogy, you can appreciate the overall purpose of Luke. Watch especially his emphasis on Jesus's title as "Son of God."

First, at the annunciation to Mary, Jesus is the "Son of God" (1:35)—and declared such by an angel. Next, at the baptism of Jesus, "when Jesus also had been baptized . . . the heaven was opened, and the Holy Spirit descended upon him in bodily form like a dove. And a voice came from heaven, 'You are my Son, the Beloved; with you I am well pleased'" (3:21–22). Once again, Jesus is Son of God—and declared such by God. Finally, Luke concludes his genealogy in 3:38 with ". . . son of

Enos, son of Seth, son of Adam, son of God." By that gene-alogy Luke draws a deliberate link between Jesus as "Son of God" and Adam as "Son of God."

Next, Luke's conjunction of the waters of baptism and Jesus as the new Adam sends us back to Genesis 1:1–2: "When God created the heavens and the earth, the earth was a formless void and darkness covered the face of the deep, while a wind from God swept over the face of the waters." That divine wind is literally the "spirit of God," *pneuma theou* in Greek, and it reappears at Jesus's baptism in Luke 3:22 as the "Holy Spirit," *to pneuma to hagion* in Greek. When you combine the waters of creation and the waters of baptism, collate the Spirit of God hovering over earth and over Jesus, and watch the title "Son of God" used for Jesus in 3:22 and for Adam in 3:38, you can easily understand Luke's theological purpose. Jesus is a new Adam, a new "Son of God," the start of a new creation, the beginning of a transfigured earth.

We recognize that theme from the theology of Paul, but there is no evidence that Luke gets it from Paul—or even knows of his letters or his theology. Paul wrote to the Cor-inthians that "'The first man, Adam, became a living being'; the last Adam became a life-giving spirit" (1 Cor. 15:45) and that "if anyone is in Christ, there is a new creation: everything old has passed away; see, everything has become new" (2 Cor. 5:17). And he told the Galatians that "a new creation is every-thing" (6:15). Luke agrees.

There is one more point to be made about the content and lo-cation of Luke's genealogy outside the Christmas story proper. It opens with this line: "Jesus was about thirty years old when he began his work. He was the son (as was thought) of Joseph son of Heli" (3:23). That phrase "Jesus . . . when he began his work" is, literally, "Jesus beginning" (*Iēsous archomenos*), in which the second word is almost an adjectival description of him. In other words, it forcibly emphasizes that, for Jesus *after his baptism by John,* there was a "beginning" (*archē*) and not simply a continuation.

We are back once more in Genesis. Creation opens there with the phrase: "In the beginning" (*archē*). Luke uses that same word for the start of Jesus's public life both at the end of his gospel ("Galilee where he began," 23:5) and in his Acts of the Apostles ("all that Jesus did and taught from the beginning," 1:1; "beginning from the baptism of John," 1:22; and "beginning in Galilee after the baptism that John announced," 10:37). Jesus "begins" as a new creation. And that transformation of the earth in Jesus was destined by God from all eternity. Genealogy is destiny.

THE GENEALOGY OF ANOTHER SON OF GOD

Even—or especially—when all those allowances are made for metaphorical mathematics and parabolic ancestry in the genealogies of Matthew and Luke, there is one final question. Why did they even bother to invent them? Why did both of them—separately, independently, and differently—create any genealogy at all?

After all, Jesus's Lukan descent from Adam is not exactly unique, since we are all so descended in biblical tradition. And, Jesus's Matthean descent from Abraham is something he held in common with all other Jews. Even descent from Abraham through David is hardly enough to make Jesus the Messiah. At most, that descent might be a necessary condition for such status, but certainly not a sufficient cause. So why, once again, did both those evangelists include a more or less invented genealogy for Jesus? In answer, we will revert to their historical context in the first century.

We Christians think of Jesus as the divine Son of God (*huios theou*) by—working backward—his resurrection, baptism, conception, and even genealogy. But there was also another human being in the Mediterranean world who was the divine Son of God (*huios theou*) by—also working backward—senatorial decree, adoption, conception, and even genealogy. We are speaking, of course, about Caesar Augustus, emperor of Rome at the time Jesus was born. And we see those genealogies of Jesus in Matthew and Luke as countergenealogies to that of Caesar Augustus.

Julius Caesar, along with his grandnephew and adopted son Octavian—the later Caesar Augustus—belonged to the Julian tribal family (*gens*). They claimed a millennium-old descent from the goddess Venus, daughter of Jupiter, and her human consort Anchises, a Trojan hero from the time of that legendary war against the Greeks. The divine son of Venus and Anchises was named Aeneas, and it is through his son, Julus, that the Julian line claimed descent.

This genealogical claim received its pseudohistorical basis from the Augustan poet Virgil in the *Aeneid,* or story of Aeneas, the foundational epic of the Roman Empire, proposed by Augustus and published by him after Virgil's death in 19 BCE. Think of Homer's *Iliad* and *Odyssey*—war followed by sea voyage—as the Old Testament of Roman imperial theology and Virgil's *Aeneid*—sea voyage followed by war—as its New Testament. And it all began at the time of the Trojan War over a thousand years before the birth of Augustus.

In the *Aeneid,* Aeneas successfully escaped the doomed city of Troy holding his aged and infirm father on his shoulder and his young son, Julus, by the hand. Protected by Venus, they eventually reached Italy, and from them, eventually, the Roman race and the Julian line descended. "From this noble line shall be born the Trojan Caesar [Augustus]," says Virgil, "who shall extend his empire to the ocean, his glory to the stars, a Julius name descended from the great Julus! Him [that is, Augustus], in days to come, shall you, anxious no more, welcome to heaven, laden with Eastern spoils; he, too, shall be invoked in vows" (286–90). The speaker there is the high god Jupiter and, after that apotheosis of the divine Augustus, "wars shall cease and savage ages soften" into peace on earth.

Most of the inhabitants of the Roman Empire were illiterate and were not reading Virgil, so that genealogical "flight from Troy" had to be communicated across the empire not in text, but in image. As an analogy, imagine this Christmas scene on fresco, mosaic, sculpture, or bas-relief, on the granite stone of an Irish cross or the stained-glass window of a European cathedral: a woman with a baby on her lap is seated on a donkey led by a man along a road. We would immediately recognize "The Flight into Egypt." So also with its Roman imperial equivalent, "The Flight from Troy."

The ubiquity and uniformity of its imagery indicates an archetypal model in the Forum of Augustus at Rome. In the center is Aeneas. He carries his infirm father, Anchises, on his left shoulder, and Anchises in turn carries their household gods (*penates*) on his lap. With his right hand Aeneas holds that of young Julus. It is not only the great image of Augustan genealogical origins; it is the supreme model of Roman patriarchal piety (*pietas*), combining both family and religion in one scene. That scene swept across the Roman Empire in the first century—you find it on a tombstone in Italy, a bas-relief in Turkey, an altar in Tunisia, to name just a few almost at

random. That bas-relief at Aphrodisias in Turkey, for example, has a fourth figure in the background. Venus's arms are
outstretched protectively around her fleeing family. Indeed—
and remember this when you think about another westward-
leading star with Matthew's Magi—it was her guiding light as
evening or morning star that showed them their path of destiny ever westward from Troy to Italy.

One note on the ancient—or modern—difficulties of ques-
tioning the historicity of divinely ordered genealogy. When he
came to tell that "Flight from Troy" story in his 142-volume
Roman history, *From the Founding of the City,* in the early 20s
BCE, the historian Livy stayed wisely careful about the man
whom the Julian house claimed, under the name of Julus, as
the founder of their name: "I will not discuss the question—
for who could speak decisively about a matter of such extreme
antiquity?" Who indeed could "speak decisively" when writing under Augustus?

Still, if you wanted to oppose and replace one Son of God
born with a millennium-plus descent from the divinely born
Aeneas, you would have to introduce an alternative Son of
God with a better than millennium-plus descent from, say, the
divinely born Isaac, as in Matthew, or, better, the divinely created Adam, as in Luke. But what is always clear is that ancient
genealogy was not about history and poetry, but about prophecy and destiny, not about accuracy, but about advertising.

CHAPTER FIVE

AN ANGEL COMES
TO MARY

This chapter is about the conception of Jesus, and our title is quite obviously appropriate for that subject. But to Mary—where? Most Christians would probably answer at Nazareth without much hesitation. But you will recall from Chapter 1 that, as their Christmas stories open, Joseph and Mary were living at Bethlehem for Matthew, but they were living at Nazareth for Luke. Afterward they moved from Bethlehem to Nazareth permanently for fear of future persecution in Matthew, but they had moved only temporarily from Nazareth to Bethlehem in Luke.

First of all, then, the angel's annunciation took place at Bethlehem for Matthew, but at Nazareth for Luke. That, however, is not the more striking difference in their two conception stories. It is that, for Matthew, the annunciation happened to Joseph, but for Luke, it happened to Mary.

Think about that for a moment. You probably have no trouble imagining an annunciation scene to Mary from its consistent portrayal in Christian art. Can you recall one painting of an annunciation to Joseph? Why was the golden luminosity of those angelic daytime annunciations to Mary never matched by the mysterious darkness of an angelic nighttime annunciation to Joseph? Luke's annunciation to Mary has wiped out completely Matthew's to Joseph in Christian imagination.

Put more broadly and bluntly, why is Matthew's entire Christmas story told from Joseph's viewpoint, while Luke's is told—as is surely more obviously intuitive—from Mary's? In simple indication of that divergence, leave aside the genealogies and look at the usage of their names in each overture:

	Name of Joseph	Name of Mary
In Matthew 1–2	8 times	3 times
In Luke 1–2	3 times	11 times

Is that emphasis on Joseph over Mary simply patriarchal presumption or male bias on the part of Matthew? And yet, as seen in our previous chapter, although Luke's genealogy is all about males as sons of males without any females mentioned, Matthew's version also mentions five females. Matthew's conception story, therefore, is a first entrance into this question about the emphasis on Joseph over Mary in Matthew.

Here is our sequence for this chapter. First, we begin—naturally after that question—with the conception story in Matthew 1:18–25. Next, we turn to the parallel version in Luke 1:26–38. Then, we consider the context within which those stories were written and heard in their first-century world. Finally, we widen that preceding section to consider how the ancients understood divine conceptions and whether the ancients took those stories literally or metaphorically.

"To Expose Her to Public Disgrace"

In giving the complete text of Matthew's conception story, we divide it into a sequence of three successive elements: *divorce, revelation,* and *remarriage*. Just notice them for the moment, and we will explain their importance as we proceed.

Divorce: Now the birth of Jesus the Messiah took place in this way. When his mother Mary had been engaged to Joseph, but before they lived together, she was found to be with child from the Holy Spirit. Her husband Joseph, being a righteous man and unwilling to expose her to public disgrace, planned to dismiss her quietly.

Revelation: But just when he had resolved to do this, an angel of the Lord appeared to him in a dream and said, "Joseph, son of David, do not be afraid to take Mary as your wife, for the child conceived in her is from the Holy Spirit. She will bear a son, and you are to name him Jesus, for he will save his people from their sins." All this took place to fulfill what had been spoken by the Lord through the prophet: "Look, the virgin shall conceive and bear a son, and they shall name him Emmanuel," which means, "God is with us."

Remarriage: When Joseph awoke from sleep, he did as the angel of the Lord commanded him; he took her as his wife, but had no marital relations with her until she had borne a son; and he named him Jesus. (1:18–25)

One minor note before we turn to our main point. We saw
in Chapter 4 that Matthew framed his genealogy of Jesus by
calling him the "Messiah" once in 1:1 and twice in 1:16–17.
Matthew begins his conception story of Jesus above by repeating that title for the fourth time. Matthew will use the title
"Messiah" again in 2:4, and that is five times in his infancy
narrative. You will recall from Chapter 2 that Matthew used
five dreams and *five* fulfillments in his overture to prepare
for the gospel as the *five* books of the New Pentateuch. You
will also recall from Chapter 4 that—whether deliberately or
accidentally—Mathew has *five* women in his genealogy. So
also here—and, again, whether deliberately or accidentally—
Matthew's overture has *five* mentions of Jesus as the Messiah.

We raise immediately one major problem in that Matthean
narrative. It is the question of Joseph's presumption that Mary
has committed adultery against his exclusive marital rights
as already established by their formal "engagement" (1:18),
which makes him "her husband Joseph" (1:19).

Why does Matthew even raise the issue of adultery? Did
Mary not tell Joseph what had happened? Did Joseph not believe her? Why did Joseph presume adultery? How did he
expect to solve it quietly within the publicity of an arranged
small-village marriage? And, since intercourse was at least
tolerated for an "engaged" couple, why did he expect anyone
to believe his accusation? We ask those questions, by the way,
not to investigate Joseph's intention as history, but Matthew's
intention as parable. They are not about Joseph, but about
Matthew. Notice, by the way, that Matthew cauterizes Joseph's
presumption of adultery even before he records it. He mentions "from the Holy Spirit" twice—once in 1:18 and again in
1:20, so that those verses frame Joseph's doubt in 1:19.

As a counterexample, the problem of possible adultery is never raised in Luke's account of Jesus's conception. Luke 1:26—like Matthew 1:18 above—starts with "a virgin engaged to a man whose name was Joseph, of the house of David. The virgin's name was Mary" (1:26). But when this engaged virgin conceives, Luke never tells us how Joseph finds out or reacts to the fact. When we next meet the couple after the angel Gabriel's annunciation to Mary, Joseph is going to Bethlehem "to be registered with Mary, to whom he was engaged and who was expecting a child" (2:5). There is no hint anywhere in Luke that Joseph had a problem with Mary's pregnancy, and thoughtful hearers or readers would simply presume that, as soon as Mary met Joseph after Gabriel's annunciation, she told him the truth and he believed her.

That is what happened, for example, with the conception of Samson in Judges 13:1–24. His mother was barren and, after a manlike angel announced her miraculous conception, "the woman came and told her husband" (13:6); he immediately believed her and wanted to ask the angel about the child's up-bringing (13:8).

Even if Matthew wanted to tell the story totally from Joseph's point of view—unlike Luke from Mary's—he could have had that angel reveal everything to him *before* Mary's conception. And if he wanted to stay patriarchal, Matthew could then have had Joseph tell Mary what would happen to her. The question therefore presses. Within the contextual matrix of Greek, Roman, and Jewish tradition of women who are virginal, sterile, or aged, why does Matthew alone raise the specter of an adulterous rather than a divine conception?

We are not simply inventing this problem in this book. That accusation of Mary's adultery was first written down toward

the end of the second century CE by the anti-Christian polemi-
cist Celsus in his book *On the True Doctrine.* (Although that
text is no longer extant, we know its contents from the third-
century rebuttal by the Christian apologist Origen.) Celsus,
and his anti-Christian Jewish source, had read Matthew—
specifically Matthew—because he speaks of Mary's "husband—the carpenter," a designation for Jesus's father created
by Matthew in 13:55 to avoid accepting it for Jesus himself
from his source in Mark 6:3. Here is the prosecuting attorney
Celsus grilling Jesus on the witness stand:

> Is it not true, good sir, that you fabricated the story of
> your birth from a virgin to quiet rumors about the true
> and unsavory circumstances of your origins? Is it not
> the case that far from being born in royal David's city of
> Bethlehem, you were born in a poor country town, and
> of a woman who earned her living by spinning? Is it not
> the case that when her deceit was discovered, to wit, that
> she was pregnant by a Roman soldier named Panthera
> she was driven away by her husband—the carpenter—
> and convicted of adultery?

The specification of the alleged adulterer as a Roman soldier
named Panthera probably derived from, first, the memory of
Syrian legionary soldiers suppressing a revolt at Sepphoris near
Nazareth around the time Jesus was born and, second, the use
of the common legionary name *Panthera* ("the Panther") as a
derisive play on *parthenos,* the Greek word for "virgin."

In other words, the accusation is that Mary's conception by
the Holy Spirit was created as a Christian cover-up for Mary's
adultery (or rape) by a pagan soldier. To the contrary, we argue
in this book that the earlier Christian claim of divine conception led to an anti-Christian accusation of adultery rather than

an earlier fact of adultery leading to a Christian claim of divine conception.

In any case, it was Matthew himself who raised the issue of Mary's possible adultery. It was Matthew himself who facilitated the anti-Christian response that a divine conception was simply a cover-up for adultery. So, once again, why did Matthew ever raise that specter of adultery (or rape) that has haunted Mary's integrity and Jesus's identity for the last two thousand years? This is where the Moses/Jesus parallelism is important for our understanding of Matthew's composition. This is the first of two major places where that parallelism is constitutive for Matthew—here concerning the *conception* of Jesus-as-Moses and later concerning the *birth* of Jesus-as-Moses (which we cover in Chapter 6).

But here is our major point. For that parallelism, Matthew does not depend on Exodus 1–2 directly, but on popular expansions of that text current in contemporary first-century Jewish tradition. In that tradition a biblical text could be retold with expansions and contractions, interpretations and explanations, in works known as *targumim,* or translations, and *midrashim,* or commentaries. Those texts, for example, often filled in answers to questions that intelligent hearers or readers might ask about an ancient text. Why this, why that, or why something else? Those expansions were the Bible retold as sermon. It is to those popular traditions that we turn next.

From Mosaic *Midrash* to Matthean Parable

What problems and questions did those popular expansions see concerning the infancy of Moses in Exodus 1–2? There were two main ones. We look at the first one concerning the *conception* of Moses in this chapter and hold the second, concerning the *birth* of Moses, until the next chapter.

According to Exodus 1–2, Pharaoh decided that the Jews resident in Egypt had become too numerous, and he tried to exterminate them first by slave labor and then by killing all newborn males. "Every boy that is born to the Hebrews you shall throw into the Nile, but you shall let every girl live" (1:22). But the very next verses report that "a man from the house of Levi went and married a Levite woman. The woman conceived and bore a son; and when she saw that he was a fine baby, she hid him three months" (2:1–2).

Here is the obvious first question. Why did those Jewish parents continue having marital intercourse if newborn male babies were doomed to certain deaths? The answer in those popular expansions is this: Amram and Jochebed, the parents of Moses-to-be, decided to *divorce* rather than bear children doomed, if male, to death. But they were instructed by a divine *revelation* to come back together in *remarriage,* since the predestined child would be their son. We look now at the extant versions of that answer.

Our basic example is a book once incorrectly attributed to the Jewish philosopher Philo and therefore known in scholarship as Pseudo-Philo's *Book of Biblical Antiquities,* or *Liber Antiquitatum Biblicarum*. It consists of an imaginative retelling of the biblical story from Adam to David, and it dates from the land of Israel around the time of Jesus. We focus here on its expansion of the infancy story of Moses as it relates to that first question about his conception.

It tells how, after Pharaoh's infanticide decree, married Jewish couples decide to *divorce* or at least abstain from marital intercourse, lest their newborn sons be killed. But one father, Amram, refuses to join that general decision and advises *remarriage* for all. Then, in a *revelation,* God rewards him for his trust by promising that Moses would be his son. Later, his and Jochebed's daughter, Miriam, gives them a similar *revelation* from a dream:

> *Divorce:* Then the elders of the people gathered the people together in mourning [and said] . . . "Let us set up rules for ourselves that a man should not approach his wife . . . until we know what God may do." And Amram answered and said . . . "I will go and take my wife, and I will not consent to the command of the king; and if it is right in your eyes, let us all act in this way."

> *Revelation 1:* And the strategy that Amram thought out was pleasing before God. And God said . . . "He who will be born from him will serve me forever."

> *Remarriage:* And Amram of the tribe of Levi went out and took a wife from his own tribe. When he had taken her, others followed him and took their own wives. . . .

> *Revelation 2:* And this man had one son and one daughter; their names were Aaron and Miriam. And the spirit of God came upon Miriam one night, and she saw a dream and told it to her parents in the morning, saying: I have seen this night, and behold a man in a linen garment stood and said to me, "Go and say to your parents, 'Behold he who will be born from you will be cast forth into the water; likewise through him the water will be dried up. And I will work signs through him and save my people, and he will exercise leadership always.' " And when Miriam told of her dream, her parents did not believe her. (9:1–10)

We have emphasized those three italicized elements, of course, because Matthew used them, as we noted above, in his parallel story of Jesus's conception in 1:18–25. That story has all three elements, but our next two examples show how some of them can be given or omitted in other versions of this story.

First, in Josephus's *Jewish Antiquities* from the end of the first century CE, there is no mention of *divorce* and *remarriage,* but a "perplexed" Amram prays to God for guidance and the *revelation* ensues:

> Amaram(es), a Hebrew of noble birth, fearing that the whole race would be extinguished through lack of the succeeding generation, and seriously anxious on his own account because his wife was with child, was in grievous perplexity. He accordingly had recourse to prayer to God. . . .

> *Revelation:* And God had compassion on him and, moved by his supplication, appeared to him in his sleep, exhorted him not to despair of the future, and told him that . . . "This child, whose birth has filled the Egyptians with such dread that they have condemned to destruction all the offspring of the Israelites, shall indeed be yours; he shall escape those who are watching to destroy him, and, reared in a marvelous way, he shall deliver the Hebrew race from their bondage in Egypt, and be remembered, so long as the universe shall endure, not by Hebrews alone but even by alien nations." (2.210–11)

Notice that the *revelation* now comes in a dream—as in Matthew. But notice especially that in this midrashic tradition the focus is on the father, Amram, as it is on Joseph in Matthew's parallel version.

Second, the alternative omission takes place in the *Targum Pseudo-Jonathan,* or *Targum of Jerusalem I.* That text has a very explicit mention of *divorce* and *remarriage,* but no *revelation:*

Divorce and Remarriage: And Amram, a man of the tribe of Levi, went and returned to live in marriage with Jochebed his wife, whom he had put away on account of the decree of Pharaoh. And she was the daughter of a hundred and thirty years when he returned to her; but a miracle was wrought in her, and she returned unto youth as she was, when in her minority she was called the daughter of Levi. And the woman conceived and bore a son at the end of six months.

We conclude with a final example, which is also as an indication of the endurance of these midrashic developments of Exodus 1–2. This is a very full version in a medieval collection known as the *Sefer ha-Zikhronot,* or *Book of Memoirs.* We have, once again, those same three classical structural elements of the story:

Divorce: When the Israelites heard this command of Pharaoh to cast their males into the river, some of the people separated from their wives, while others remained with them. . . . When, however, the word of the king and his decree became known respecting the casting of their males into the river, many of God's people separated from their wives, as did Amram from his wife.

Prophecy: After the lapse of three years the Spirit of God came upon Miriam, so that she went forth and prophesied in the house, saying, "Behold, a son shall be born to my mother and father, and he shall rescue the Israelites from the hands of the Egyptians."

Remarriage: When Amram heard his young daughter's prophecy he took back his wife, from whom he had separated in consequence of Pharaoh's decree to destroy all the

male line of the house of Jacob. After three years of separation he went to her and she conceived.

In this version, even Amram follows the general *divorce,* then
the *revelation* comes to Miriam, and the *remarriage* ensues.
Furthermore, at the birth of Moses, "The whole house was at
that moment filled with a great light, as the light of the sun
and the moon in their splendour."

Our conclusion is that Matthew very, very deliberately
based Jesus's conception closely on those midrashic versions of
Moses's conception already current in the first century. That
explains his emphasis on divine control through dreams and
prophecies, which, as you will recall, extends from the conception story in a fivefold repetition throughout Matthew 1–2.
It also explains his exclusive focus on the male and paternal
viewpoint, with Joseph as the new Amram even though, after
those five women in the genealogy, you might have expected
more mention of Mary. It explains his sequence of *divorce* in
1:18–19, *revelation* in 1:20–23, and *remarriage* in 1:24.

Finally, it explains the byproduct of that creative parallelism, namely, Joseph's mistaken presumption of Mary's adultery, with its unfortunate legacy in ancient polemics as well
as modern commentaries. Matthew needed to create the sus-
picion of adultery in order to provide a reason for Joseph to
seek a divorce, thus setting in motion that midrashic pattern
of *divorce, revelation,* and *remarriage.* And all of this is part of
Matthew's "Jesus is the new Moses" motif.

"The Virgin's Name Was Mary"

Both Matthew and Luke agree that Mary was an engaged
virgin when she conceived Jesus. And both agree that her

pregnancy was not from Joseph but from "Holy Spirit," that is, the Spirit of God. Since they agree on those two aspects of Jesus's conception and since there is a general scholarly consensus that Matthew and Luke are independent of one another, those two details must come from earlier tradition.

(That virginal *conception* of Jesus should not be confused with the Roman Catholic doctrine of his virginal *birth*—with Jesus coming from Mary's womb like sunlight through the glass of a medieval cathedral window. That is not found in either Christmas story. Neither should it be confused—and it is regularly confused in the media—with the "immaculate conception." That is another Roman Catholic doctrine meaning that Mary herself was conceived without the stain [Latin *macula*] of original sin—as was Jesus also. That is also not found in either Christmas story.)

Mary as a Virgin. Matthew 1:18 starts with this verse: "When his mother Mary had been engaged to Joseph, but before they lived together, she was found to be with child from the Holy Spirit." Luke also starts with "a virgin engaged to a man whose name was Joseph, of the house of David. The virgin's name was Mary" (1:26). And then Luke continues: "The Holy Spirit will come upon you, and the power of the Most High will overshadow you; therefore the child to be born will be holy; he will be called Son of God" (1:35). Here is the full text of Luke 1:26–38 to compare with the one from Matthew 1:18–25 given above:

> In the sixth month the angel Gabriel was sent by God to a town in Galilee called Nazareth, to a virgin engaged to a man whose name was Joseph, of the house of David. The virgin's name was Mary. And he came to her and said, "Greetings, favored one! The Lord is with you."

But she was much perplexed by his words and pondered what sort of greeting this might be. The angel said to her, "Do not be afraid, Mary, for you have found favor with God. And now, you will conceive in your womb and bear a son, and you will name him Jesus. He will be great, and will be called the Son of the Most High, and the Lord God will give to him the throne of his ancestor David. He will reign over the house of Jacob forever, and of his kingdom there will be no end." Mary said to the angel, "How can this be, since I am a virgin?" The angel said to her, "The Holy Spirit will come upon you, and the power of the Most High will overshadow you; therefore the child to be born will be holy; he will be called Son of God. And now, your relative Elizabeth in her old age has also conceived a son; and this is the sixth month for her who was said to be barren. For nothing will be impossible with God." Then Mary said, "Here am I, the servant of the Lord; let it be with me according to your word." Then the angel departed from her.

Why does that common pre-Matthean and pre-Lukan tradition mention that Mary was a virgin? If you respond, "Because she was," I rephrase my question. Why was that important enough to mention? What is at stake in the claim of virginity even or especially within the protocols of a divine conception? For either Jewish or Greco-Roman tradition would a divine conception be any less divine if it involved a woman with prior children?

The answer seems quite obvious, and many Christians could probably give it immediately. Mary had to be a virgin as a fulfillment of Isaiah 7:14. That is clear and explicit in

Matthew's assertion that, "All this took place to fulfill what had been spoken by the Lord through the prophet [Isaiah]: 'Look, the virgin shall conceive and bear a son, and they shall name him Emmanuel,' which means, 'God is with us'" (1:25). But here are some questions that need to be asked before accepting that reply. Was that claim that Mary's virginal conception came from Isaiah 7:14 already present in the common tradition used independently by Matthew and Luke? It is certainly in Matthew, as just seen, but is it also in Luke? If not, was it Matthew himself who created that prophetic fulfillment by connecting Mary's virginity to Isaiah 7:14?

First, there is no evidence that Luke knows any connection between Mary's virginity and that text in Isaiah 7:14. But, you object, what about when Gabriel says to the "virgin" (*parthenos*) Mary in Luke 1:31 that she "will conceive . . . and bear a son, and . . . name him Jesus"? Is that not at least an implicit reference to Isaiah 7:14, where the prophet tells King Ahaz of Judah that "the young woman (*parthenos*) is with child and shall bear a son, and shall name him Immanuel"?

No, not at all, because that phrase is intended by Luke as one more in a long series of very deliberate parallels between the conception stories of Jesus and John the Baptizer in Luke 1–2 (as you can see in Appendix 2).

One comment on that general parallelism before continuing with the question of Mary's virginity in Luke 1–2. As just seen, Matthew draws parallels between Jesus and Moses in order to exalt Jesus over Moses in Matthew 1–2. Similar parallels are drawn to exalt Jesus over John the Baptizer in Luke 1–2. But Jesus is not simply the new John for Luke as Jesus is the new Moses for Matthew. The point is that—for Luke—John is the symbol, synthesis, conclusion, and consummation of the Old Testament. John was conceived—to conclude the Old Testament—in an aged and barren mother, but Jesus was born—to start the New Testament—of a virginal mother.

We return now to Mary's virginity in Luke. Against the general background of his Jesus/John parallelism—with fuller detail available in Appendix 2—look at this specific parallelism between the conception annunciations of Jesus and John over these five points:

John	Jesus
1. But the angel said to him,	The angel said to her,
2. "Do not be afraid, Zechariah,	"Do not be afraid, Mary,
3. for your prayer has been heard.	for you have found favor with God.
4. Elizabeth will bear you a son,	And now, you will . . . bear a son,
5. and you will name him John."	and you will name him Jesus."
(1:13)	(1:31)

In other words, Luke in 1:31 is not referring back to the birthing and naming in Isaiah 7:14, but to the birthing and naming of John from his own 1:13. And, beyond that parallelism, of course, Luke looks back before Elizabeth and John to Sarah and Isaac: "Your wife Sarah shall bear you a son, and you shall name him Isaac" (Gen. 17:19).

In conclusion, that reference to Isaiah 7:14 is present in Matthew, but *not* in Luke and, therefore, *not* in the tradition about Mary's virginal conception they inherited independently of one another. It is best seen as Matthew's own creation, a creation necessitated by his need for exactly *five* prophetic fulfillments (and *five* angelic dream messages) in Matthew 1–2 as overture to the five great discourses of Jesus in Matthew 3–28. We will see much more about those prophecies in Chapter 8.

Mary as a Model. We turn now to another striking element in that annunciation story in Luke 1:26–38, an emphasis on—in this order—Jesus *and* Mary. This appears clearly in the overall structure of the *conversation*—we use that term deliberately—between the angelic Gabriel and the virginal Mary:

Address by Gabriel to Mary	1:28	1:30–33	1:35–37
Response from Mary to Gabriel	1:29	1:34	1:38

In the *address* section of that dialogue, therefore, the identity of Jesus is built up over the three parallel passages:

"The Lord is with you." (1:28)	"You will conceive in your womb and bear a son, and you will name him Jesus. He will be great, and will be called the Son of the Most High, and the Lord God will give to him the throne of his ancestor David. He will reign over the house of Jacob forever, and of his kingdom there will be no end." (1:31–33)	"The Holy Spirit will come upon you, and the power of the Most High will overshadow you; therefore the child to be born will be holy; he will be called Son of God." (1:35)

Jesus is "Son of God," but that God is identified twice as the "Most High," that is, as the God of the Jewish and biblical tradition. That would hardly have been necessary to emphasize unless there was another Son of God not so related within the general context. He is, of course, the emperor Caesar Augustus at the time of Jesus's conception, and also the contemporary Roman emperor at the time of Luke's Christmas story.

That triadic structure also allows Luke a secondary emphasis on Mary as the perfect Christian. She is "the favored [*literally,* graced] one" who has found "favor [*literally,* grace] with God." And her obedient response to God's favor/grace is this: "Here am I, the servant of the Lord; let it be with me according to your word."

Luke's vision of Mary receiving Christ as the first and perfect Christian may be seen most clearly in the way he rephrases his Markan source concerning her in this example:

Mark 3:31–35	*Luke 8:19–21*
Then his mother and his brothers came; and standing outside, they sent to him and called him. A crowd was sitting around him; and they said to him, "Your mother and your brothers and sisters are outside, asking for you." And he replied, "Who are my mother and my brothers?" And looking at those who sat around him, he said, "Here are my mother and my brothers! Whoever does the will of God is my brother and sister and mother."	Then his mother and his brothers came to him, but they could not reach him because of the crowd. And he was told, "Your mother and your brothers are standing outside, wanting to see you." But he said to them, "My mother and my brothers are those who hear the word of God and do it."

In Mark Jesus's physical family is rejected in favor of a spiritual one of all those who do "the will of God." But in Luke that physical family—and especially Mary from 1:38—is the model for all "who hear the word of God and do it."

Finally, it is obvious why Luke insists that Jesus's conception was not just from God, but from a *virginal* mother. That was necessitated by his parallelism and exaltation of Jesus's conception over that of John the Baptizer, as detailed in Appendix 2. But, since a *virginal* conception of Jesus is both pre-Matthean and pre-Lukan, the wider question still presses. If that earlier Christian tradition did not take Mary's virginity from Isaiah 7:14, why did it emphasize the *virginity* of Mary—emphasize not just a divine conception but a virginal divine conception?

As with so many of our questions about the content of the Christmas stories, we go for answers into that general context of their first-century Jewish and Roman world. And here we look specifically at what we might have expected about divine conceptions from that contemporary matrix.

Divine Conception in Jewish Tradition

What about divine conception in Judaism? And since we have just seen in great detail the Old Testament model behind Matthew 1–2, what about the Old Testament model behind Luke 1–2?

In biblical tradition a transcendentally predestined child is conceived and born to barren and/or aged parents. Actually, such an event is far more manifestly miraculous and clearly divine than any sort of virginal conception outside of marriage or prior to it. The claim of virginal conception could be a simple mistake or even a lie. But clearly postmenopausal conception and birth are open—at least in theory and even in story—to overt verification.

Luke 1:6–7 says of Zechariah and Elizabeth, "Both of them were righteous before God, living blamelessly according to all the commandments and regulations of the Lord. But they had no children, because Elizabeth was barren, and both were getting on in years." Luke's major models for that situation are the classically Jewish stories about Isaac's conception by Sarah and Abraham in Genesis 17–18 and Samuel's conception by Hannah and Elkanah in 1 Samuel 1–2.

Sarah. The birth of Isaac is the archetypal story of a divinely created conception in the biblical and Jewish tradition—from a barren wife *and* aged parents. Abraham says, "I continue childless" in Genesis (15:2). His wife, Sarah, "bore him no children" since, as she says, "the Lord has prevented me from bearing children" (16:1–2). Then follow twin accounts of the conception of Isaac in Genesis. The earlier one is the Jahwist tradition (or J) from around 900 BCE, now in Genesis 18; the later one is the Priestly (or P) tradition of around 500 BCE, now in Genesis 17. But they both agree on these four sequential elements as the core of the story.

First, the *apparition:* "The Lord appeared to Abraham" is present in both accounts. But in 17:1 Abraham heard a voice saying, "I am God Almighty," while in 18:2 he "looked up and saw three men standing near him."

Next, the *promise,* and even though it is made to the father, the mother at least gets mentioned: "As for Sarah your wife . . . I will give you a son by her. I will bless her, and she shall give rise to nations; kings of peoples shall come from her" (17:15–16); and "I will surely return to you in due season, and your wife Sarah shall have a son" (18:10).

Then, comes the *objection*—the laughter. In the Priestly version: "Abraham fell on his face and laughed, and said to himself, 'Can a child be born to a man who is a hundred years old? Can Sarah, who is ninety years old, bear a child?'" (17:17). But the Jahwist version gives that laughter—more against Abraham than God?—to Sarah:

> Now Abraham and Sarah were old, advanced in age; it had ceased to be with Sarah after the manner of women.

So Sarah laughed to herself, saying, "After I have grown old, and my husband is old, shall I have pleasure?" The Lord said to Abraham, "Why did Sarah laugh, and say, 'Shall I indeed bear a child, now that I am old?'"... But Sarah denied, saying, "I did not laugh"; for she was afraid. He said, "Oh yes, you did laugh." (18:11–13, 15)

The point of the *objection* and of all that laughter is, of course, to underline the miraculously divine intervention involved in this conception by extraordinarily aged parents.

Finally, there is the *repetition,* as God repeats the divine covenantal promise: "No, but your wife Sarah shall bear you a son, and you shall name him Isaac" (17:19); and again: "At the set time I will return to you, in due season, and Sarah shall have a son" (18:14). That promise is fulfilled when "Sarah conceived and bore Abraham a son in his old age" (21:2).

All of that is to emphasize that aged and barren parents could only conceive by a miraculous divine intervention. And, had you been there, it would all have been empirically verifiable at least with regard to age and sterility.

Hannah. The birth of Samuel is another such story in the biblical and Jewish tradition. In 1 Samuel 1–2, Hannah and Elkanah are a barren couple who are not explicitly aged, although it is repeated twice that, "year by year" (1:3, 7), "the Lord had closed her womb" (1:5–6). So Hannah vows to God: "If only you . . . will give to your servant a male child, then I will set him before you as a nazirite until the day of his death. He shall drink neither wine nor intoxicants, and no razor shall touch his head" (1:11). The priest Eli promises that God will answer her prayer for a child and, after discreetly noted marital intercourse (1:18–19), "Hannah conceived and bore a son. She named him Samuel" (1:20).

Then, as she had vowed, Hannah dedicates the infant Samuel to God as an ascetic or nazarite (from the Hebrew for "a separated one") according to the protocols of Numbers 6:1–21. She then breaks into a long canticle that begins: "My heart exults in the Lord; my strength is exalted in my God" (2:1). Once again, you can see that story model behind Luke's account of John the Baptizer as one who, by divine command, "must never drink wine or strong drink" (1:15) and Mary's triumphant canticle, the Magnificat, which begins, "'My soul magnifies the Lord, and my spirit rejoices in God my Savior" (1:46–47). But more later on those parallels.

Why, then, to repeat our question, did that earlier tradition behind both those Christmas stories insist not just on a divine conception, but on a virginal divine conception? Why not follow Jewish tradition of at least sterile if not aged parents?

The only reason we can suggest is part of a deliberate exaltation of the New Testament over the Old Testament. That is certainly how Luke takes it. John the Baptizer, as the end of the Old Testament, is born of barren and aged Elizabeth (1:7), but Jesus, as the start of the New Testament, is born of a virginal Mary (1:27, 34). And, as we see next, exaltation over its contemporary matrix applies likewise to one very specific contemporary Roman tradition.

DIVINE CONCEPTION IN ROMAN TRADITION

In Greco-Roman tradition a transcendentally predestined child is conceived by divine intercourse with a human being—either female goddess with human male or male god with human female. The most important one from that matrix is the conception of Octavian, whose parents were Atia and Octavius and who would one day be the emperor of Rome and the god Augustus.

Around 120 CE, Suetonius, imperial secretary and palace gossip, wrote *The Lives of the Caesars,* and in the section *The Deified Augustus* he recorded this omen:

> A few months before Augustus was born a portent was generally observed at Rome, which gave warning that nature was pregnant with a king for the Roman people; thereupon the senate in consternation decreed that no male child born that year should be reared; but those whose wives were with child saw to it that the decree was not filed in the treasury, since each one appropriated the prediction to his own family. (94.3)

That attempt to destroy the boy born to be king by killing all contemporary male children is, of course, a standard folk-loric tradition, which we saw already in the story of Pharaoh in Exodus 1–2, which was carried over into Jesus's story in Matthew 1–2.

Suetonius then records the divine conception of Octavian, later to be Augustus. He cites it from the *Theologoumena (Discourses on the Gods)* by Asclepias of Mendes in Egypt, which probably means that it originated when Octavian was there after the battle of Actium, between 31 and 29 BCE, in mopping-up operations against Antony and Cleopatra:

> When Atia had come in the middle of the night to the solemn service of Apollo, she had her litter set down in the temple and fell asleep, while the rest of the matrons also slept. On a sudden a serpent glided up to her and shortly went away. When she awoke, she purified herself,

as if after the embraces of her husband, and at once there
appeared on her body a mark in colors like a serpent, and
she could never get rid of it; so that presently she ceased
ever to go to the public baths. In the tenth month after
that Augustus was born and was therefore regarded as
the son of Apollo. (94.4)

But Suetonius only furnishes that information after he had
fully detailed Augustus's life and accomplishments up to and
including the portents that warned of his death. By then, as
it were, readers might be ready to believe a divine conception!

The story of Octavian's divine conception is modeled on
the earlier and similar conceptions for the Greek general
Alexander, imperial conqueror of the Persians, and for the
Roman general Scipio Africanus, imperial conqueror of the
Carthaginians. Augustus was destined to out-conquer them
both. We already saw a similar modeling of Jesus's conception
story on that of Moses by Matthew

Whether we look for elucidation on divine conceptions to
the general Jewish tradition of barren and aged parents or to
that specific story about Octavian, the reason for an emphasis
on virginity in the pre-Matthean and pre-Lukan Christmas
story is in order to exalt the divine conception of Jesus over all
others—especially over that of Augustus himself.

In Jewish and biblical tradition, ordinary marital intercourse takes place between aged and barren parents—even if
conception is thereafter divinely miraculous. In Greco-Roman
tradition, and notable in that Augustan story above, divine intercourse takes place in a physical manner, so that it was necessary for Atia to purify herself "as if after the embraces of
her husband." Even with Greco-Roman divine conceptions,

the male god engages in intercourse, so that the human mother is no longer a virgin after conception.

What pre-Matthean and pre-Lukan Christianity claimed was that Mary remained a virgin before, during, and after *conception* (not *birth*)—and that made her divine conception different from and greater than all others.

Anti-Christian polemicists often argue that Christianity simply copied its story from those of other contemporary divine conceptions, and so it is irrelevant. Pro-Christian apologists often insist that nothing *exactly* like Luke 1:26–38 occurred in ancient tradition, and so is unique. Both extremes are incorrect, because Christianity described the divine *and virginal* conception of Jesus precisely to exalt it over all those other ones—and especially over that of Caesar Augustus. Is it, by the way, ungracious to note that the Holy Spirit requested Mary's agreement to her divine pregnancy, but Apollo accorded Atia no such courtesy?

In any case, virginity, sterility, longevity, or anything else one can imagine are simply ways of emphasizing, underlining, and "proving" that the conception was divine. It is that divine conception that counts. It is the theology of the child and not the biology of the mother that is at stake.

In a Pre-Enlightenment World

Among the ancients, did all or most or many or only some individuals take stories of divine conceptions literally and historically, or metaphorically and parabolically? Did they even press that distinction as relentlessly as we so often do? Or were they quite capable of understanding the meaning of those stories without even asking about their mode?

We begin with two preliminary warnings. First, in an ancient world, where understanding of the microscopic interaction between ovum and sperm was almost two millennia in the future, "conception" was a rather mysterious affair. The ancients knew, of course, that human intercourse was normally necessary and that both female and male fluids existed, but the dominant metaphors for conception as "sowing the seed" and for birthing as "opening the womb" leave much room for puzzle, miracle, and mystery.

Second, it is neither helpful nor accurate to exalt Jewish or Christian divine conceptions over their pagan equivalents. Conception by human-divine interaction was a cultural given in that pre-Enlightenment world, so that, although any specific example might be denied, the general possibility was presumed. The exact mechanics depended on how literal the writer's imagination or the hearers' understanding was. Pro-Christian apologists could argue that pagan divine conceptions *did* not happen, and anti-Christian polemicists could argue back that Christian ones *did* not happen, but both sides presumed they *could* happen. Even to argue that *ours* are divine while *yours* are demonic simply derides actuality without denying possibility.

Granted those warnings, how can we tell when people in a pre-Enlightenment world—where divine interventions were generally accepted as possible—took those stories of divine conception as literal or as metaphorical? Here are a few examples of how at least some writers thought about that problem.

In the first century CE, the Roman historian Livy commented on two very famous divine conceptions in his history of Rome, *From the Founding of the City*. You will recall him from Chapter 4 prudently refusing to judge for or against Augustus's alleged descent from Aeneas. Speaking of those divine conceptions of Alexander and Scipio, he declared them "equally empty and absurd," but he also notes that "Scipio himself never said a word to diminish belief in those marvels; on the contrary, he tended to strengthen it by skillfully and deliberately refusing either to deny or openly to affirm their truth" (26.19).

In the second century CE, the historian and biographer Plutarch wrote *Parallel Lives* about famous Greeks and Romans and, among them, a *Life of Numa,* the legendary second king of Rome after Romulus in the 600s BCE. He tells how "the goddess Egeria loved him and bestowed herself upon him, and it was his communion with her that gave him a life of blessedness and a wisdom more than human." Plutarch notes similar stories from other traditions about mortals "who were thought to have achieved a life of blessedness in the love of the gods." But this is his concluding judgment: "There is some reason in supposing that Deity . . . should be willing to consort with men of superlative goodness, and should not dislike or disdain the company of a wise and holy man. But that an immortal god should take carnal pleasure in a mortal body and its beauty, this, surely, is hard to believe" (4.1–3).

In the third century CE, the philosopher Iamblichus wrote *Life of Pythagoras* about that earlier philosopher from the sixth century BCE. Iamblichus quotes a claim that "Pythagoras was the son of Apollo" and a human mother, but he then denies it and explains how the rumor started. Pythagoras's father, Mnesarchus, impregnated his wife, Pythais, and then went away on business before he learned of her condition. At Delphi, Apollo told him that "his wife was now pregnant, and would bring forth a son surpassing in beauty and wisdom all that ever lived, and who would be of the greatest advantage to the human race"—that, by the way, is a perfect job description for a human being divinely conceived. In other words, Pythagoras's greatness was foretold by Apollo, but Pythagoras's conception by Apollo "is by no means to be admitted." Still, Iamblichus continues, "no one can doubt that the soul of Pythagoras was sent to humanity from the empire of Apollo, either being an attendant on the God, or co-arranged with him in some other more familiar way" (2).

For Greeks, Romans, Jews, and Christians in that ancient and pre-Enlightenment world, interaction of the human and divine——however imagined, described, or micromanaged—could produce a child who would bring transcendental benefits to the human race. And, of course, that logic also worked in reverse—a transcendental benefactor must have had a divine conception. If male, that child could be termed "Son of God"—a relational metaphor just like Word of God, Lamb of God, or Image of God. In fact, as we just saw, Luke's genealogy could describe not only Jesus as "Son of God" (1:35), but Adam as "Son of God" (3:38).

Finally, then, it is unwise to imagine that those pre-Enlightenment ancients told incredible histories, which we post-Enlightenment moderns have learned to deride. It is wiser to realize that they used powerful metaphors and told profound parables, which we have taken literally and misunderstood badly. And that is a warning against either accepting or rejecting metaphor literally and parable factually in texts from a pre-Enlightenment world. Whether taken literally or metaphorically, a divine conception was their way of asserting an individual's transcendental character and extraordinary gifts to the human world. We may, of course, deny that ancient explanation for extraordinary individuality, but we must also admit that we moderns have no better one to take its place.

It would be wiser, therefore, to presume that the ancients were as wise as we moderns are—when we are both wise—and as dumb as we moderns are—when we are both dumb. But, whether taken literally or metaphorically, historically or parabolically, any claim of a divine conception—whether from virginal, barren, or aged parents—claims that this child has brought or will bring extraordinary or transcendental benefits to the human race. And, therefore, the proper question is not about the biology of the mother, but the destiny of the child. What is that destiny and, once you know it, are you willing to commit your life to it? To Caesar the Augustus, for example, *or* to Jesus the Christ?

CHAPTER SIX

IN DAVID'S CITY OF BETHLEHEM

We saw in a preceding chapter that the Christmas stories of Matthew and Luke disagree on the location of Jesus's conception by the Holy Spirit. It was Bethlehem for Matthew, but Nazareth for Luke. They both agree, however, on the location of his birth in Bethlehem and, furthermore, they both agree that Joseph was a descendant of David.

Matthew says that, "Jesus was born in Bethlehem of Judea" (2:1) and that Joseph is the "son of David" (1:20), and so, therefore, "Jesus the Messiah [is] the son of David" (1:1). Luke brings those two elements together: "Joseph also went from the town of Nazareth in Galilee to Judea, to the city of David called Bethlehem, because he was descended from the house and family of David. He went to be registered with Mary, to whom he was engaged and who was expecting a child. While they were there, the time came for her to deliver her child" (2:4–6).

Matthew and Luke agree, therefore, that Jesus was the new David. But, recall that, as we already saw in Chapter 5 and will see again in this chapter, Jesus is for Matthew the new Moses. Matthew's Christmas story combines, in other words, Jesus as new Moses and as new David, so that Jesus will "save his people from their sins" (1:21) nonviolently rather than from their enemies violently.

Since Matthew and Luke agree independently on those two points about Jesus—that he was descended from David's lineage and born in David's city—those must come from an earlier tradition than either of their Christmas stories. And, in fact, we find both of those points elsewhere in the New Testament.

First, Paul, in opening his letter to the Romans, speaks of "the gospel concerning his [God's] Son, who was descended from David according to the flesh" (1:3). Second, John records the crowd's discussion of Jesus's messianic status with this interchange: "Others said, 'This is the Messiah.' But some asked, 'Surely the Messiah does not come from Galilee, does he? Has not the scripture said that the Messiah is descended from David and comes from Bethlehem, the village where David lived?'" (7:41–42). This is a typical instance of Johannine irony. He presumes that Jesus was born at Bethlehem and, therefore, the crowd's ignorance confirms what they deny. Jesus *is* the Messiah, and he *was* born in Bethlehem. Paul and John indicate that common Christian tradition that Jesus was the Davidic Messiah and was—whether literally or metaphorically—born in Bethlehem.

While we are on this subject of agreements between Matthew and Luke in their overtures, here is a fuller list of their Christmas story agreements:

	Matthew 1–2	Luke 1–2
Mary was engaged to Joseph.	1:18	1:27; 2:5
Mary conceived while a virgin.	1:18, 25	1:27, 34
Mary conceived by God's Holy Spirit.	1:18, 20	1:35
Jesus was named by God.	1:21	1:31
Jesus was "to save" or was "Savior."	1:21	1:47, 69; 2:11
Jesus was the Davidic Messiah.	1:1, 16–17, 20	1:27, 32, 69
Jesus was born at David's city of Bethlehem.	2:1	2:4, 11
Jesus was born under Herod the Great.	2:1	1:5
Mary, Joseph, and Jesus live in Nazareth.	2:22–23	2:39, 51

As we saw at the start of Chapter 5, Matthew uses the title of Messiah five times in his Christmas story. And—whether deliberate or accidental there—and here once again—he also mentions Bethlehem five times:

1. "Jesus was born in Bethlehem of Judea." (2:1)

2. "They told him, 'In Bethlehem of Judea.'" (2:5)

3. "And you, Bethlehem, in the land of Judah . . ." (2:6)

4. "Then he sent them to Bethlehem." (2:8)

5. "He sent and killed all the children in and around Bethlehem." (2:16)

Luke mentions Bethlehem twice, once when Jesus's parents go there in 2:4 and again when the shepherds go there in 2:15. What is fascinating, however, is that, although their common tradition furnished them with information about a Bethlehem birth, it did not tell them how Jesus happened to be born in Bethlehem. How was Jesus of Nazareth born in Bethlehem?

Here is the sequence for this chapter. First, we look at the original David to see what made him the once and future king of Israel, so we can determine how Jesus could be the new David. Next, we discuss the birth of Jesus in Matthew's Christmas story. And you will not be surprised to be back once more with his model from those *midrashim* about the birth of Moses. Then, we look at the birth story of Jesus in Luke with special attention to titles for Jesus such as "Lord" and "Savior" in that account. That involves a focus on those same titles for Roman emperors from Caesar Augustus onward. Finally, we focus on two more words in Luke's overture, and indeed in all of Luke-Acts—*gospel* and *peace*—within that same context of Roman imperial theology. Our question is this: if Caesar Augustus and his kingdom of Rome and Jesus Christ and his kingdom of God both promise a transcendental peace for earth, so that their *end* is the same, must not the difference between them be in their *means* to get to that *end*? What, then, are those divergent *means* for peace on earth?

THE ONCE AND FUTURE DAVID

You will recall, from the end of Chapter 3, that there was no completely unified consensus about the identity of God's intermediary for the eschatological transformation, or Great Divine Cleanup of the World. But insofar as there was *any* popular agreement, it was that the Anointed One would be a Davidic Messiah, that is, a new David, who would establish justice and peace for God's people. His character, activity, and salvific success had to be like David's, but to be born of David's lineage or born in David's city were probably quite negotiable. But, before looking at Jesus as the new David, who or what exactly was the old David?

About a millennium before the time of Jesus, Philistine invaders struck the southern coastal plain of Israel with iron weaponry, swift chariotry, and unified leadership. In responding to this lethal threat, the tribes of Israel first chose an unsuccessful defender in Saul, who was badly defeated by the invaders. Then, ignoring Saul's dynastic pretensions, they chose a very successful defender in David, who finally defeated the Philistine advances. That story is told—in a serene combination of historical fact and romantic fiction—in 1–2 Samuel and 1 Kings 1:1–2:11. And, of course, "David was the son of an Ephrathite of Bethlehem in Judah, named Jesse" (1 Sam. 17:12). David was born in Bethlehem.

But apart from David's personal success historically as a military leader and king of Israel, it is especially his dynastic images as filtered theologically through the royal psalms and prophetic promises that we see visions of the new David, the new Anointed One—"Messiah" in Hebrew, "Christ" in Greek—who would establish justice and righteousness, peace and security for his people.

In Psalm 2, for example, on the day of his royal enthronement in Jerusalem, a descendant of David is the "anointed" (2:2), "king" (2:6), and "son" of God, because, "today I [God] have begotten you" (2:7). God also promises him, "I will make the nations your heritage, and the ends of the earth your possession" (2:8). That is surely a promise more in the theological future that the historical present.

In another Psalm God says, "I have found my servant David; with my holy oil I have anointed him" (89:20), and, "He shall cry to me, 'You are my Father, my God, and the Rock of my salvation!' I will make him the firstborn, the highest of the kings of the earth" (89:26–27). Furthermore, once again, God promises, "I will crush his foes before him and strike down those who hate him" (89:23).

You can read this prophetic medley as a commentary on that once and future Davidic king and especially on his attributes and activities. Notice how the future arrival of the new David is "on that day" or on "days that are surely coming" or "in those days":

> On that day I will raise up the booth of David that is fallen, and repair its breaches, and raise up its ruins, and rebuild it as in the days of old. (Amos 9:11)

> His authority shall grow continually, and there shall be endless peace for the throne of David and his kingdom. He will establish and uphold it with justice and with righteousness from this time onward and forevermore. (Isa. 9:7)

> Then a throne shall be established in steadfast love in the tent of David, and on it shall sit in faithfulness a ruler who seeks justice and is swift to do what is right. (Isa. 16:5)

> The days are surely coming, says the Lord, when I will raise up for David a righteous Branch, and he shall reign as king and deal wisely, and shall execute justice and righteousness in the land. (Jer. 23:5)

> In those days and at that time I will cause a righteous Branch to spring up for David; and he shall execute justice and righteousness in the land. (Jer. 33:15)

In reading those texts, we ask you to recall what we said in Chapter 3 about messianic expectations from texts around the time of Jesus. We drew attention there to two questions concerning those expectations for God's anointed intermediary. First, was he to be human or transcendent? And, second, was he to be violent or nonviolent?

To answer those questions, we turn to *The Scepter and the Star* by John J. Collins of Yale University. It is a very thorough and helpful survey of messiahs in ancient literature. Collins focuses, despite other "minor" understandings of the term "messiah" around the time of Jesus, on this "common core" or "dominant note":

> This concept of the Davidic messiah as the warrior king who would destroy the enemies of Israel and institute an era of unending peace constitutes the common core of Jewish messianism around the turn of the era. . . . There was a dominant notion of a Davidic messiah as the king who would restore the kingdom of Israel, which was part of the common Judaism around the turn of the era.[1]

The Davidic Messiah as a warrior king is not, therefore, just one option among many messianic understandings and expectations. It is, rather, the basic one. And that, of course, raises this immediate problem:

> Although the claim that he [Jesus of Nazareth] is the Davidic messiah is ubiquitous in the New Testament, he does not fit the typical profile of the Davidic messiah. This messiah was, first of all, a warrior prince, who was to defeat the enemies of Israel. . . . There is little if anything in the Gospel portrait of Jesus that accords with the Jewish expectation of a militant messiah.[2]

We cannot explain that discrepancy by taking the "common core" or "dominant note" of a violent Davidic Messiah as

"Jewish" and that of a nonviolent Davidic Messiah as "Christian." At least for some Jews at the start of the first century CE that understanding of the warrior Davidic Messiah underwent a profound mutation in interaction with their experience of Jesus himself. *For some Jews, in other words, Jesus was a nonviolent Davidic Messiah.* It is necessary, therefore, to accept fully the profound mutation that Davidic messianism underwent within Judaism in that first century.

We are back, in other words, with those two questions about the Messiah from our Chapter 3. Would the Messiah be human or transcendent? Would the Messiah be nonviolent or violent? For those Jews who accepted Jesus as the Davidic Messiah—and whom we would later call Christians—the answer to those two questions was quite clear. As the Davidic Messiah or new David, Jesus was human *and* transcendent *and* nonviolent. His establishment of "justice and righteousness"—as promised by those prophets above—would be not by violence, but by nonviolence.

MESSIAH AND KING OF THE JEWS

In Matthew's Christmas story the Magi are being led toward Jesus's birthplace by their miraculous star. So you might wonder why they stop in Jerusalem and ask for directions. But, hold that question for a moment, and notice this juxtaposition of questions and titles in 2:2–4:

Magi to Herod:	"Where is the child who has been born King of the Jews?"
Herod to Advisers:	"Where [is] the Messiah to be born?"

The Messiah, for Matthew, is King of the Jews. But what is most striking is that Matthew never uses that title again until Pilate judges and executes Jesus at the end of his gospel: the governor asks, "Are you the King of the Jews?" (27:11); the soldiers mock, "Hail, King of the Jews" (27:29); and the indictment on the cross reads, "This is Jesus, the King of the Jews," (27:37). That title never appears, by the way, in Luke or the other gospels except during those same execution processes. Why does Matthew alone make this very deliberate juxtaposition of Herod and Pilate?

It is Roman power alone that designated and supported Herod the Great as "King of the Jews." In 40 BCE, Marc Antony "determined then and there," according to Josephus's *Jewish War,* "to make him King of the Jews" (1.282). Since Antony and Octavian were still allies at that date—a decade before Actium—they combined to get the Senate's agreement, and then they both "left the senate-house with Herod between them, preceded by the consuls and other magistrates, as they were to offer sacrifice and to lay up the decree in the Capital" (1.285).

It is therefore very significant that Matthew calls Jesus by the pointedly anti-Roman title "King of the Jews" (2:2), and not, say, "king of Israel." That is the title used, for example, by the evangelist John at the start of Jesus's public life: "Nathanael replied, 'Rabbi, you are the Son of God! You are the King of Israel!'" (1:49); and also by Mark at the end: "Let the Messiah, the King of Israel, come down from the cross now, so that we may see and believe" (15:32).

The use of that title "King of the Jews" in Matthew 2:2–4 is, therefore, another overture-to-gospel theme. Roman-appointed Herod seeks to kill, and Roman-appointed Pilate succeeds in killing Jesus, the messianic King of the Jews. The shadow of Roman imperial execution hangs already and immediately over the birth of Jesus. Put another way, the clash between Jesus the Messiah and Caesar Augustus the emperor started right from the birth of Jesus.

"WISE MEN FROM THE EAST CAME TO JERUSALEM"

We turn now to the birth of Jesus in Matthew's Christmas story. You will recall from Chapter 5 that in Matthew's story Jesus's conception was created in parallelism with and in exaltation over Moses's conception as reflected in contemporary popular accounts. As seen there, those popular versions in *targumim* (translations) and *midrashim* (commentaries) expanded creatively on the bare-bones version in Exodus 1–2. Matthew does exactly the same with the story of Jesus's birth as he did previously with that of his conception.

The Birth of Moses in the Midrashim

In Chapter 5, the three units of the parallelism between the conceptions of Moses and Jesus were the *divorce, revelation,* and *remarriage*. Those expansions intended to answer this obvious question about the conception of Moses in Exodus 1–2. If their male children were to be killed, why did parents continue in wedlock and intercourse?

We have a similar situation here in this chapter concerning the *birth parallelism* of Moses and Jesus. The obvious question about the birth of Moses in Exodus 1–2 is this. How did it happen that Moses was born just after that decree of genocide by Pharaoh? Did he just happen to get born at the wrong time and place? What about divine providence?

In answer to that question, the popular traditions claimed that it was precisely in order to kill Moses that the general newborn-male infanticide took place. It was not that Moses just happened to be born at the wrong time and in the wrong place. Instead, Pharaoh had a mysterious *dream* that caused *fear* within the court. The *interpretation* of his counselors foretold the birth of a Jewish male infant who would grow to greatness as a dangerous threat to Egypt. And so, precisely in order to kill that predestined child, this Moses-to-be, Pharaoh gave the command to slaughter all the newborn male infants of the Jews.

The model for those expansions of Exodus 1–2, by the way, is also biblical. It derives from the book of Daniel, where you have that same sequence of *dream, fear,* and *interpretation.* First, in Daniel 2, the king of Babylon, Nebuchadnezzar, "dreamed such dreams that his spirit was troubled and his sleep left him. So the king commanded that the magicians, the enchanters, the sorcerers, and the Chaldeans be summoned to tell the king his dreams" (2:1–2). But only Daniel could, with divine assistance, interpret his dream. Those same three elements occur for Daniel himself with the *dream* in 7:1–14, the *fear* in 7:15, and the *interpretation* in 7:16–27. And, as with the three elements of *divorce, revelation,* and *remarriage* in the Moses/Jesus conception parallelism, so also here with the three elements of *dream, fear,* and *interpretation* in the birth parallelism of Moses and Jesus, we expect and get creative variation rather than strict uniformity.

We looked at four texts for the conceptions of Moses and Jesus, but have only three texts for their births, since Pseudo-Philo does not have any expansion on that latter subject. So this time we begin with the *Targum Pseudo-Jonathan,* or *Targum of Jerusalem I,* on Exodus 1–2:

> *Dream:* And Pharaoh told that he, being asleep, had seen in his dream, and, behold, all the land of Egypt was placed in one scale of a balance, and a lamb, the young of a sheep, was in the other scale; and the scale with the lamb in it overweighed.

> *Interpretation:* Forthwith he sent and called all the magicians of Mizraim, and imparted to them his dream. Immediately Jannis and Jambres, the chief of the magicians, opened their mouth and answered Pharaoh: A certain child is about to be born in the congregation of Israel, by whose hand will be destruction to all the land of Egypt.

Pharaoh's "chief magicians" are identified as Jannes and Jambres, and those names are another typical example of midrashic, or sermonic, expansions. Confronted by the power of the adult Moses in Exodus 7:11, "Pharaoh summoned the wise men and the sorcerers; and they also, the magicians of Egypt, did the same by their secret arts." No names are given there, but 2 Timothy in the New Testament says that "Jannes and Jambres opposed Moses" (3:8). By then or later, they even had their very own book, the *Book of Jannes and Jambres.* *Midrash* is a growth industry.

You will have noticed, however, that the targumic translation mentions *dream* and *interpretation,* but no intervening reaction of *fear.* Here is another version of that tradition from, once again, Josephus's late-first-century *Jewish Antiquities:*

> *Prophecy:* While they were in this plight, a further incident had the effect of stimulating the Egyptians yet more to exterminate our race. One of the sacred scribes—persons

with considerable skill in accurately predicting the future—announced to the king that there would be born to the Israelites at that time one who would abase the sovereignty of the Egyptians and exalt the Israelites, were he reared to manhood, and would surpass all men in virtue and win everlasting renown.

Fear: Alarmed thereat, the king,

Advice: on this sage's advice, ordered that every male child born to the Israelites should be destroyed by being cast into the river. (2.205–6)

Notice that, for Josephus, *prophecy* replaces *dream* and, with *fear* intervening, *advice* replaces *interpretation*. For his Greco-Roman audience, Josephus prefers to speak about prophetic sages rather than royal nightmares.

Finally, the most complete version is, once again, in the *Sefer ha-Zikhronot,* or *Book of Memoirs.* In that story, the *fear* element applies not just to Pharaoh, as in Josephus, but to all his servants:

Dream: In the 130th year after the Israelites had gone down to Egypt, Pharaoh dreamt a dream. While he was sitting on the throne of his kingdom he lifted up his eyes, and beheld an old man standing before him. In his hand he held a pair of scales as used by merchants. The old man then took the scales and, holding them up before Pharaoh, he laid hold of all the elders of Egypt and its princes, together with all its great men, and, having bound them together, placed them in one pan of the scales. After that he took a milch goat, and, placing it on the other pan, it outweighed all the others. Pharaoh then awoke, and it was a dream.

Fear: Rising early next morning, he called all his servants, and told them the dream. They were sorely frightened by it,

Interpretation: and one of the king's eunuchs said, "This is nothing else than the foreboding of a great evil about to fall upon Egypt." On hearing this the king said to the eunuch, "What will it be?" And the eunuch replied, "A child will be born in Israel, who will destroy all the land of Egypt. If it is pleasing to the king, let the royal command go forth in all the land of Egypt that every male born among the Hebrews should be slain, so that this evil be averted from the land of Egypt."

That triadic structure of *dream, fear,* and *interpretation*—with Exodus 1–2 filled out from Daniel 2, 4, and 7—holds firm across a millennium with, of course, specific details added or omitted in any given version.

The Birth of Jesus and the Mosaic Midrashim

Our proposal in Chapter 5, on Jesus's conception, and in this present Chapter 6, on his birth, is that the general structure of the popular traditions about Moses's infancy gave Matthew the basic outline for his Moses/Jesus parallelism. That explains, as we saw already, why Matthew must tell the infancy story from the viewpoint of Joseph and not of Mary (as in Luke). He is watching consistently the Mosaic parallelism, with its emphasis on the father, Amram, and not on the mother, Jochebed. Here is how Matthew fashions the birth story of Jesus to be parallel to that of Moses:

Magi: In the time of King Herod, after Jesus was born in Bethlehem of Judea, wise men from the East came to

Jerusalem, asking, "Where is the child who has been born King of the Jews? For we observed his star at its rising, and have come to pay him homage.". . . And having been warned in a dream not to return to Herod, they [the Magi] left for their own country by another road. (2:1–2, 12)

Fear: When King Herod heard this, he was frightened, and all Jerusalem with him. (2:3)

Interpretation: And calling together all the chief priests and scribes of the people, he inquired of them where the Messiah was to be born. They told him, "In Bethlehem of Judea." (2:4–5)

You will notice, of course, that Matthew's parallelism does not match the *dream* of Pharaoh with a *dream* of Herod. Why does he make that change?

The Magi Stop for Directions

Matthew's five dreams in 1:20; 2:12, 13, 19, 22 are all salvific messages from God to good people, not harmful suggestions to evil ones. The addition of the Magi allows him to start his story not with Herod's dream, but with their advent. And, thereafter, that dream can be relocated from Herod to them (the other dreams are all for Joseph). Thus, Matthew's dreams remain positive divine commands without injecting a negative royal nightmare among them. But that emphasizes Matthew's own creation of those eastern astrologers, the Magi from Mesopotamia, who come to pay homage to the infant Jesus.

Furthermore, you can understand now why, despite God's guiding star, the Magi stop to see Herod at Jerusalem to get directions. In order to avoid a *dream* for Herod, they must take its place in the Mosaic parallelism, and so they start the process toward *fear* and *interpretation*.

The Magi are the literary descendants of "the magicians, the enchanters, the Chaldeans [Babylonians], and the diviners" who appear repeatedly as opponents in Daniel 1:20; 2:2; 4:7; 5:7. But Matthew now depicts these Gentiles as pro-Jesus, while Herod "and all Jerusalem with him" are anti-Jesus (2:3). That is a very ironic reversal. But for Matthew Jesus is savior not just of Jews, but of Gentiles. Those are "his people" whom he will "save from their sins" (1:21). So we go, once more, from overture to gospel and, indeed, from start to conclusion of that Matthean gospel. The words of the departing Jesus to his disciples in Matthew are: "Go therefore and make disciples of all nations" (28:19).

The Magi follow a westward-leading star from Mesopotamia to Judea. On the one hand, from within the Jewish matrix, we know that the following oracle was understood of the awaited Messiah both before and after the time of Jesus: "I see him, but not now; I behold him, but not near—a star shall come out of Jacob, and a scepter shall rise out of Israel; it shall crush the borderlands of Moab, and the territory of all the Shethites" (prophecy of Balaam, Num. 24:17). In that application, the Messiah is the Star and the Scepter who will conquer the enemies of Israel. But, of course, for Matthew the star is not Jesus himself, but what leads one to Jesus.

On the other hand, therefore, this westward-guiding star is Matthew's most obvious allusion to Roman imperial theology and the birth story of the Julian tribal family from Venus and Anchises through Aeneas to Julus and thereafter. As you will recall from Chapter 4, it was the star of Venus, as first to appear in evening or last to disappear in morning, that lead the Trojan refugees westward to Italy. But now it is another, a replacement westward-leading star, that brings the Magi to Jerusalem with this question for Herod: "Where is the child who has been born King of the Jews? For we observed his star at its rising, and have come to pay him homage" (2:2).

Next, it is often noted that the "slaughter of the innocents" is completely in character for the suspicious if not paranoid Herod. That, of course, simply proves that Matthew intends a realistic parable and not necessarily a factual history—like Jesus saying that "a man was *going down* from Jerusalem to Jericho" in the parable of the good Samaritan in Luke 10:30. Jericho is about three thousand feet below the level of Jerusalem. That motif of killing all males to get one newborn looks from Herod back to Pharaoh and not from Herod back to history. It is, in fact, the linchpin of Matthew's parallelism for the birth stories of Moses the Great and Jesus the Greater.

Finally, in Matthew, the major difference between the birth stories of Moses and Jesus is not in the conception or the birth, but in the escape. And this difference is hugely and deliberately ironic. Escape for Moses is *from* Egypt, but for Jesus it is *to* Egypt. The place of past doom and death for Moses has become the place of refuge and life for Jesus.

"A Decree Went Out from Emperor Augustus"

We turn now from the birth of Jesus in Matthew to that in Luke. You will recall from Chapter 1 that, while Matthew had Jesus's parents living in Bethlehem when their child was born, Luke had to get them there from Nazareth, where—as far as he was concerned—they had previously been living. So Luke's problem was how to get them from Nazareth to Bethlehem, and this is his five-point solution:

1. In those days a decree went out from Emperor
   Augustus that all the world [Greek *oikoumenē*]
   should be registered.

2. This was the first registration and was taken while
   Quirinius was governor of Syria.

3. All went to their own towns to be registered.

4. Joseph also went from the town of Nazareth in
   Galilee to Judea, to the city of David called
   Bethlehem, because he was descended from the
   house and family of David.

5. He went to be registered with Mary, to whom
   he was engaged and who was expecting a child.
   (2:1–5)

That solution is as traditionally famous as it is historically incorrect on each of its five major points. And, unfortunately,
arguments for and against their accuracy have completely obscured Luke's purpose and intention in creating them.

1. Roman imperial theology always talked of a predestined rule over the "whole world" and the "inhabited earth"
(*oikoumenē*)—and not just over Italy or even the Mediterranean. Three examples will suffice.

First, from texts: at the start of Virgil's *Aeneid,* Jupiter de-
crees that, "I set no bounds in space or time but have given
empire without end ... [to] the Romans, lords of the world,
and the nation of the toga" (1.278–83). Second, on coins: those
minted by Octavian to pay down his victorious legions and
pay off the defeated ones after Actium, for example, show
him as a divine being with his foot on the globe of the earth.
Third, with statues: one modeled on Zeus from Olympias

shows Augustus with that globe in his hand surmounted by the winged goddess Victory.

But, taken literally, Caesar Augustus never did and never could have ordered a census of the entire Roman Empire, let alone the entire inhabited world, all at one time. Taken metaphorically, of course, conquering for occupation and then counting for taxation was simply Rome's manifest destiny and imperial program for "the whole world." We even wonder if Luke, who knew quite a lot about the Roman Empire and its processes, could ever have intended that sentence literally?

2. In 6 CE Rome removed Herod the Great's son Archelaus as its indirect, or client, ruler of Judea and replaced him by direct Roman control. As was usual in such a situation, there followed the "first registration," that is, census for taxation, of that southern Jewish homeland. This was conducted by the Syrian governor Publius Sulpicius Quirinius, who was sent out in 6 CE with the express purpose of performing that duty. Luke mentions that census again in his Acts of the Apostles and adds correctly that "Judas the Galilean rose up at the time of the census and got people to follow him; he also perished, and all who followed him were scattered" (5:37).

But Luke had already dated the conceptions of John and Jesus within "the days of King Herod of Judea." Matthew agreed that it was "in the time of King Herod" that "Jesus was born in Bethlehem of Judea" (2:1). Indeed, we have to imagine Jesus's birth in Matthew as much as two years before Herod's death in March/April of 4 BCE. Herod "sent and killed all the children in and around Bethlehem who were two years old or under, according to the time that he had learned from the wise men" (2:16). He thought, in other words, that Jesus could have been born up to two years before the Magi finally arrived in Jerusalem.

Here, then, is the heart of the matter with regard to the historical accuracy of Luke 2:1–5. The birth of Jesus under the rule of Herod the Great, which ended in 4 BCE, cannot have taken place under the census of Quirinius, which started in 6 CE.

3. The Roman taxation census is best known from the copious records in the dry sands of Egypt. It was done by one's own household (*idia*) and absence from home to avoid the census was a crime. The only relocation ever required was to be "at home," that is, in one fixed abode, for the count. You were counted where you lived, worked, and paid your taxes. What is described by Luke in that third point would have been, then or now, a geographical impossibility, a bureaucratic nightmare, and a fiscal disaster.

4. Joseph lived in the north under Herod Antipas of Galilee, and any taxes would have been paid there and not in the south, which alone had passed under direct Roman control. Quirinius had no direct authority over Galilee.

5. Mary would not have been required to appear personally with Joseph even if we imagine a situation where he himself had to do so. Registration by household was the responsibility of the head of the household.

All of that must be openly admitted and never evaded with any specious or dishonest arguments. But saying it is not enough. There is still and always this question. What was Luke attempting to say when he got his facts so wrong?

First, in general, the many contacts between Jesus and world leaders or between Christianity and world history in Luke-Acts intend to emphasize that, as he has Paul say at trial before the Roman governor Festus and the Herodian king Agrippa II in Acts, "this was not done in a corner" (26:26). That is why he connects the birth of Jesus with "the Emperor Augustus" and why he begins the narrative of his public life with: "In the fifteenth year of the reign of Emperor Tiberius, when Pontius Pilate was governor of Judea, and Herod was ruler of Galilee, and his brother Philip ruler of the region of Ituraea and Trachonitis, and Lysanias ruler of Abilene, during the high priesthood of Annas and Caiaphas" (3:1–2). Jesus and earliest Christianity are, in other words, historically located, imperially dated, and cosmically significant events.

Second, in this particular case, there is a very deliberate Lukan connection between the birth of Jesus and an alleged worldwide census for taxation "decreed by the Emperor Augustus." We return to that below, and Luke's intention behind that juxtaposition will become clearer in the rest of this chapter when we watch how key Lukan terms like "Lord," "Savior," "gospel," and "peace" are taken from references to Caesar the Augustus and applied to Jesus the Christ.

Finally, we emphasize this point. No argument—however correct—that Caesar Augustus never did or could have ordered a single taxation census of the entire world should make us forget, for example, an image like that on the so-called *Gemma Augustea*. On that large and beautiful onyx cameo from the early first century CE, now in a Viennese museum, a woman who symbolizes *Oikoumenē* is shown crowning the divine, seminude Augustus with a wreath of oak leaves for saving the whole inhabited earth. If, then, Luke was literally incorrect in 2:1, he was very much metaphorically correct.

"Let Us Go Now to Bethlehem"

We begin by picking up the Christmas story in Luke from 2:1–5 above, where Joseph and the pregnant Mary have arrived in Bethlehem. This is how Luke describes Jesus's birth, something Matthew did not do:

While they were there, the time came for her to deliver her child. And she gave birth to her firstborn son and wrapped him in bands of cloth, and laid him in a manger, because there was no place for them in the inn. (2:6–7)

What exactly is Luke describing with that "inn" and "manger"? Those two terms fit well with what we know from the much later Ottoman Empire, whose ruined caravansaries (literally, "camel-caravan-palaces") still border the Silk Road in central Turkey. Imagine, therefore, a more primitive version of such a structure in Bethlehem.

It had a gated enclosure with a central courtyard for the animals; around that were covered rooms without doors from which you could keep an eye on those animals, and toward the back were regular closed rooms. Luke mentions those details not to hint at poverty for the family, but simply because—like any good parabler—he knows how to be accurately and creatively realistic.

Luke imagines Bethlehem crowded with Davidic descendants for the imperial taxation census. All the closed and private rooms were gone, and so were all the covered and semiprivate ones around the open courtyard. Jesus, therefore, is born among the animals in that open courtyard and laid in one of their feeding troughs.

The story continues:

In that region there were shepherds living in the fields, keeping watch over their flock by night. Then an angel of the Lord stood before them, and the glory of the Lord shone around them, and they were terrified. But the angel said to them, "Do not be afraid; for see—I am bringing you good news of great joy for all the people:

to you is born this day in the city of David a Savior, who is the Messiah, the Lord. This will be a sign for you: you will find a child wrapped in bands of cloth and lying in a manger.". . . . So they went with haste and found Mary and Joseph, and the child lying in the manger. When they saw this, they made known what had been told them about this child; and all who heard it were amazed at what the shepherds told them. But Mary treasured all these words and pondered them in her heart. The shepherds returned, glorifying and praising God for all they had heard and seen, as it had been told them. (2:8–12, 16–20)

In citing that passage, we deliberately omitted Luke 2:13–15 in order to return to it in much greater detail as the final section of this chapter and part.

Lord. Notice the two mentions of "the Lord" in that passage. The first one, "the glory of the Lord" (2:9), refers to God as the Lord. But the second one, "the Messiah, the Lord" (2:11), refers to Jesus. That theologically motivated double usage appeared earlier in Luke's Christmas story when Mary called herself "the servant of the Lord" (1:38), meaning of God, and Elizabeth called her "the mother of my Lord" (1:43), meaning of Jesus. For Luke "the Lord" is both God and God as revealed in Jesus.

Shepherds. Why did Luke choose shepherds for his angelic revelation? One reason is, as we mentioned in Chapter 2, his concern for those whom society has marginalized. Luke alone, for example, has Jesus quote Isaiah 61:1–2: "The Spirit of the Lord is upon me, because he has anointed me to bring good news to the poor. He has sent me to proclaim release to the captives and recovery of sight to the blind, to let the oppressed go free, to proclaim the year of the Lord's favor" (4:18–19). And, later, the Lukan Jesus repeats that "the poor have good news brought to them" (7:22).

Another reason why Luke chose shepherds to receive God's message about the birth of Jesus is that David was himself a shepherd. This is repeated several times in 1 Samuel 16:11–17:34. When Samuel comes to make David king, for example, he asked his father, Jesse, "Are all your sons here?" Jesse answered, "There remains yet the youngest, but he is keeping the sheep" (16:11). And, again, "David went back and forth from Saul to feed his father's sheep at Bethlehem" (17:15).

Format. The structure of the angelic message to the shepherds follows what Luke had already established with those to Zechariah and Mary. That repetition is another indication of Luke's compositional creativity in his Christmas story:

	To Zechariah	To Mary	To the Shepherds
Angel	1:11	1:26–28	2:9a
Fear	1:12	1:29	2:9b
Reassurance	1:13a	1:30a	2:10a
Message	1:13b–17	1:30b–35	2:10b–11
Sign	1:18–20	1:36–37	2:12

Titles. The heart of the angelic message is that cluster of titles that accompanies the announcement of Jesus's birth: "To you is born this day in the city of David a Savior, who is the Messiah, the Lord" (2:11). You will recall that the formal titles used by Matthew for Jesus are, "Messiah" and "King of the Jews" (2:2–4). In this cluster of three titles, Luke agrees on "Messiah," but frames it with "Savior" and "Lord." We turn now to consider those two titles within the context of *Judaism within the Roman Empire.*

WHO IS LORD AND SAVIOR OF THE WHOLE WORLD?

Matthew and Luke agree, as seen already, that Jesus was the Davidic Messiah. Matthew, as also seen already, emphasized the anti-Roman aspect of that title by equating it with "King of the Jews," a title that made Rome-appointed Herod seek to kill him and Rome-appointed Pilate succeed. Luke qualifies that same title of Messiah by framing it with two other titles in the angelic message to the shepherds, "Savior" and "Lord" (2:11). Those are also pointed directly against Rome—but how exactly?

Lord. Both God and Jesus are Lord (*kyrios*) as just seen in Luke's Christmas story, and throughout the New Testament. Think, for example, of Paul's great proclamation: "Even though there may be so-called gods in heaven or on earth—as in fact there are many gods and many lords—yet for us there is one God, the Father, from whom are all things and for whom we exist, and one Lord, Jesus Christ, through whom are all things and through whom we exist" (1 Cor. 8:5–6); or the one when he was in chains in a Roman prison: "Jesus Christ is Lord, to the glory of God the Father" (Phil. 2:11); or that most succinct formulation "Jesus is Lord" (1 Cor. 12:3; Rom. 10:9). So, if "Jesus as Lord" incarnates "God as Lord" within the context of Christian Judaism, it also rejects "Caesar as Lord" within the context of Roman imperialism.

It is now about one hundred years since Adolf Gustav Deissmann, professor of New Testament exegesis at the University of Berlin, published his great book *Light from the Ancient East*. He recognized clearly the confrontational purpose of taking a title like "the Lord" from Caesar Augustus and giving it to Jesus the Christ.

On the one hand, "lord" was an ordinary title used by slaves to masters or students to teachers. But used simply as "the Lord" it meant the emperor, especially from Caesar Augustus onward, just as, for example, "der Führer" simply means "the leader" in German (where all nouns are capitalized), but eventually designated Adolf Hitler as the supreme and only leader. In that context to have called Christ "der Führer" would have meant death in Dachau.

Think of just this one example from Luke himself at the start of Paul's defense before Roman and Herodian authorities in Acts. "I found that he had done nothing deserving death," said Festus the governor to Agrippa the king, "and when he appealed to his Imperial Majesty [*Sebaston*], I decided to send him. But I have nothing definite to write to our sovereign [*tō kyriō*] about him" (25:25–26). They are presumably speaking of the emperor Nero, but he is identified only as "Sebastos" and "the Lord." Sebastos is, as mentioned in Chapter 3, the Greek for "Augustus" and means "The One Who Is to Be Worshiped" (from *sebomai,* "to worship").

"Most important of all," wrote Deissmann, "is the early establishment of a polemical parallelism between the cult of Christ and the cult of Caesar in the application of the term *kyrios,* 'lord.'"[3] But, unfortunately, Deissmann—writing in a Germany already heading for imperial disaster—did not discuss what was involved in that confrontation between the lordship of Caesar and the lordship of Christ. It was, as we see in the rest of this chapter, between peace through violent victory with Caesar *versus* peace through nonviolent justice with Christ.

Savior. In the Old Testament, Isaiah addresses the "God of Israel, the Savior" (45:15). Then, as with "Lord," so also with "Savior"—it is a title for *both* God and Jesus in certain New Testament texts. But, with the exception of John 4:42, where

Jesus "is truly the Savior of the world," Luke alone uses the title "Savior" in the gospels. He also uses it in Acts: "God exalted Jesus at his right hand as Leader and Savior" (5:31) and "God has brought to Israel a Savior, Jesus, as he promised" (13:23). But, once again, if "Jesus as Savior" incarnates "God as Savior" within the context of Christian Judaism, it also rejects "Caesar as Savior" within the context of Roman imperialism.

Luke had already used that title twice in his Christmas story before the angelic usage to the shepherds—once for God and once for Jesus. In her Magnificat, Mary "rejoices in God my Savior" (1:47), and Zechariah's Benedictus praises the God who "has raised up a mighty savior [*literally,* a horn of salvation] for us in the house of his servant David" (1:69). But think now of Roman imperial theology and how Augustus "saved" the Roman Empire from civil-war suicide, as summarized in Chapter 3, and how he was then upgraded and celebrated as "Savior" of the world. Here are three examples—one in a poem and two more on inscriptions.

The contemporary poet Propertius generally preferred love poetry to war poetry, but even he rhapsodized in his *Elegies* about that salvific victory of Augustus off Cape Actium. He has the god Apollo leave his native island of Delos and take his stand above Octavian's flagship. "He spoke: 'O savior of the world . . . Augustus . . . now conquer at sea: the land is already yours: my bow battles for you'" (4.6.37–39). The god Apollo—who had conceived him—names Augustus as Savior of the World. That is, of course, salvation by victory.

Myra of Lycia, on the southern coast of western Turkey, is where Paul changed ships on his way to Roman imprisonment according to Luke in Acts 27:5. The city's inhabitants dedicated an inscription to the "divine Augustus Caesar, son of a god, imperator of land and sea, the benefactor and savior of the whole world." If you move northward around the south-western curve of Turkey's Aegean coast from ancient Myra, you come to Halicarnassus in Caria. Here is an even more effusive inscription from that city:

> Since the eternal and immortal nature of everything has bestowed upon mankind the greatest good with extraordinary benefactions by bringing Caesar Augustus in our blessed time the father of his own country, divine Rome, and ancestral Zeus, savior of the common race of men, whose providence has not only fulfilled but actually exceeded the prayers of all. For land and sea are at peace and the cities flourish with good order, concord and prosperity.

Augustus is, once again, not just Savior of Rome, but Savior of Humanity. Notice, however, that final sentence about "land and sea are at peace." We turn now, in conclusion, to focus on that *peace* and to ask what type of savior and mode of salvation will bring peace to our earth.

Whose Is the Gospel of Peace on Earth?

In citing the angelic message to the shepherds in Luke 2:8–20 above, we deliberately held this central—and inserted—section until now:

> Suddenly there was with the angel a multitude of the heavenly host, praising God and saying,
>
> > *"Glory to God in the highest heaven,*
> > *and on earth peace among those whom he favors!"*
>
> When the angels had left them and gone into heaven, the shepherds said to one another, "Let us go now to

Bethlehem and see this thing that has taken place, which the Lord has made known to us." (2:13–15)

The Peace of God

The above is the correct translation of the Greek in 2:14 rather than the King James Version's "and on earth peace, goodwill toward men." That is incorrect, and even more so is the contemporary version we hear every Christmas: "and on earth peace to men of goodwill [toward one another]." That is simply bad translation and, for Christians, bad theology as well. We turn now to discuss the location, format, and, especially, the theology of that mini-canticle in 2:14 within those frames of 2:13 and 2:14.

You know by now that Luke usually operates with single divine messengers in his Christmas story: to Zechariah (1:11–20), to Mary (1:26–38), and to the shepherds (2:9–13). You can also see from our citation above how Luke integrates this mini-hymn into his composition about an angelic message to the shepherds with the key words "angel" and "heavenly host" at the start (2:13) and "heaven" and "shepherds" at the end (2:15) of his insertion. Luke clearly wants this pre-Lukan poem integrated into the midst of his own announcement of the birth of Jesus.

In this two-strophe poem, each sentence has three concepts to be taken within this parallelism (although this is not the present Greek word order):

glory	→	in heaven	→	to God
		and		
peace	→	on earth	→	to humans of [God's] favor

What about that final word, "favor" or "goodwill" (Greek *eudokia*)? In this poetry, peace is only for those humans "of—God's—goodwill," that is, of God's preference, choice, and election. Notice how that word adds a final qualification to the balanced triad of glory/peace, heaven/earth, and God/humans, so that a mention of God occurs—directly or indirectly—at the end of each verse. But that qualification raises a problem.

Although Luke quotes the mini-canticle from another source, he modifies its theology or, at least, a possible misunderstanding of its theology. If that final qualification about "God's favor" might seem to emphasize an exclusivity of divine predestination, Luke deliberately counteracts that understanding both before and after he inserts the unit.

Before that insertion, the individual angel had announced "good news of great joy for *all the people*" (2:10). Not just to a predestined some, but to all the people. After the insertion, in the Nunc Dimittis, the next and final canticle of Luke 1–2, Simeon takes the infant Jesus in his arms and announces God's "salvation, which you have prepared in the presence of *all peoples,* a light for revelation to the Gentiles and for glory to your people Israel" (2:30–32). Even more clearly here, "all peoples" include both Jews and Gentiles.

So, granted that Luke has to emphasize that divine inclusivity, why does he want this pre-Lukan poem precisely at this point? The answer is that it allows him to bring together two of his most important concepts—gospel and peace. To understand the importance of that combination for Luke, we go—before continuing with him—into its context within Roman imperial theology. The contrast here is between the birthdays of Caesar the Augustus and Jesus the Christ, the nativity of two saviors, each claiming the gospel about the new creation of a peaceful world.

The Gospel of Caesar Augustus's Peace

If you continue northward again along the Aegean coast of modern Turkey from ancient Halicarnassus, mentioned above, you come to ancient Priene, just south of Ephesus, where, in Chapter 3, we saw that temple dedicated, in Greek, to THE AUTOCRAT CAESAR, THE SON OF GOD, THE GOD SEBASTOS.

We look here at another inscription from Priene, which is now in Berlin's Pergamon Museum. It is, in many ways, an extraordinary inscription and the most significant one for seeing the confrontation between early Christian and imperial Roman theology. It concerns the very subject of this book— *the good news about the birthday of a divine child who will save the world from destruction by establishing permanent peace.*

Almost immediately after the battle of Actium, Paulus Fabius Maximus, governor of the Roman province of Asia Minor, offered a golden crown for the best proposal for adequately honoring Augustus. About twenty years later he won the contest with his own proposal:

[It is a question whether] the birthday of the most divine Caesar is more pleasant or more advantageous, the day which we might justly set on a par with the *beginning of everything,* in practical terms at least, in that he restored order when everything was disintegrating and falling into chaos and gave a new look to *the whole world,* a world which would have met destruction with the utmost pleasure if Caesar had not been born as a common blessing to all. For that reason one might justly take this to be the *beginning of life and living*, the end of regret at one's birth. . . . It is my view that all the communities should have one and the same New Year's Day, the birthday of the most divine Caesar, and that on that day, 23rd September, all should enter their term of office.

Notice the words we have italicized. Augustus's birthday is— "in practical terms"—a new creation. It is "the beginning of everything . . . the beginning of life and living." It has saved "the whole world" from descending into chaos and all from wishing they had never been born.

By 9 BCE, the League of Asian Cities accepted the governor's suggestion and thereby made Augustus Lord not only of place, but of time as well:

> Since the providence that has divinely ordered our exis-
> tence has applied her energy and zeal and has brought to
> life the most perfect good in Augustus, whom she filled
> with virtues for the benefit of mankind, bestowing him
> upon us and our descendants as a *savior*—he who put
> an end to war and will order *peace,* Caesar, who by his
> *epiphany* exceeded the hopes of those who prophesied
> *good tidings* [*euaggelia*], not only outdoing benefactors of
> the past, but also allowing no hope of greater benefac-
> tions in the future; and since the birthday of the god first
> brought to the world the *good tidings* [*euaggelia*] residing
> in him. . . . For that reason, with good fortune and safety,
> the Greeks of Asia have decided that the New Year in all
> the cities should begin on 23rd September, the birthday
> of Augustus . . . and that the letter of the proconsul and
> the decree of Asia should be inscribed on a pillar of white
> marble, which is to be placed in the sacred precinct of
> Rome and Augustus.

We have again italicized those key words—"epiphany," "savior," "peace," and especially "good tidings" (or "gospel," *euaggelia*)—

connected with Augustus's birth, which was greater than any good news remembered from the past or imagined for the future.

(In that same year, 9 BCE, a magnificent Altar of Peace was dedicated in Rome's Campus Martius. It was consecrated not just to the Pax Romana but, more precisely, to the Pax Augustana. It is, then and now, the *Ara Pacis Augustae,* the Altar of Augustan Peace.)

But it is especially the incarnation of Roman imperial theology in the birth of Augustus, as summarized in that Priene text, that is the Roman matrix for the birth of Jesus in Luke 1–2. That is why the Lukan challenge to it comes not just from a single angel, but from "a multitude of the heavenly host" (2:13). We return now to that conjunction of *gospel* and *peace* in Luke-Acts.

The Gospel of Jesus Christ's Peace

The Greek noun *euaggelion* (singular) or *euaggelia* (plural) is composed of *eu* ("good") and *aggelion* ("news" or "message"). Thence came the Old English word *god-spel* ("good message")—combining *god,* meaning "good," with *spel* (akin to spiel), meaning "news" or "message"—from which we get *gospel.*

Luke, however, only uses that noun *euaggelion,* or "gospel," twice in all of Luke-Acts, but he uses the verb "to gospel" (*euaggelō*) twenty-five times; it is one of his favorite terms. That repeated usage is obscured by the fact that the same Greek verb is given several different translations in English:

"To proclaim the good news" (14 times; Luke 3:18; 4:43; 16:16; Acts 5:42; 8:4, 12, 25, 35, 40; 11:20; 14:7, 21; 15:35; 16:10)

"To bring the good news" (8 times; Luke 1:19; 2:10; 4:18; 7:22; 8:1; 9:6; Acts 13:32; 14:15)

"To tell the good news" (2 times; Luke 20:1; Acts 17:18)

"To preach the good news" (1 time; Acts 10:36)

Despite that diversity in translation, Luke's consistent verb is (literally) *to evangelize* or *to gospel,* that is, *to proclaim the gospel*.

Furthermore, the content of that *gospel-ing* is variously cited in Luke-Acts. In the Christmas story, the gospel content is the conception (1:19) and birth (2:10) of Jesus. Thereafter, in Luke, it is "the kingdom of God" (4:43; 8:1; 16:16). In Acts it is "Jesus as the Messiah" (5:42), "the kingdom of God" (8:12), "Jesus" (8:35), "peace by Jesus Christ—he is Lord of all" (10:36), "the Lord Jesus" (11:20), "what God promised to our ancestors" (13:32), "the word of the Lord" (15:35), and "Jesus and the resurrection" (17:18). And, when he uses the noun in Acts 20:24, the gospel content is "God's grace."

Luke combines *(to) gospel* and *peace* twice. We have just cited one instance in Acts 10:36: "You know the message he [God] sent to the people of Israel, preaching peace by Jesus Christ— he is Lord of all." But the most interesting conjunction is in his Christmas story and that message to the shepherds:

The single angel: "I am bringing you good news of great joy for all the people." (2:10)

The angelic host: "Glory to God in the highest heaven, and on earth peace among those whom he favors." (2:14)

Precisely by inserting that pre-Lukan hymn in his angelic message to the shepherds, Luke was able to combine *(to) gos-*

pel and *peace* along with an emphasis that peace comes not from earth, but from heaven to earth. And the theme of *peace* continues through Luke-Acts.

First, that theme began even earlier in the Christmas story when Zechariah proclaimed, in his Benedictus canticle, that Jesus was the dawn light "to guide our feet into the way of peace" (1:79) and Simeon announced, in his Nunc Dimittis canticle, that, with the advent of Jesus, he was now ready to die "in peace" (2:29). Next we see it when Jesus tells his disciples: "Whatever house you enter, first say, 'Peace to this house!' And if anyone is there who shares in peace, your peace will rest on that person; but if not, it will return to you" (10:5–6).

Then, on what we call Palm Sunday, Luke makes changes to his Markan source that are very significant for his understanding of Christian peace. Compare, for example, the anti-triumphal entry of Jesus into Jerusalem in Mark and Luke:

Mark 11:9–10	*Luke 19:37–38*
Then those who went ahead and those who followed were shouting, "Hosanna! Blessed is the one who comes in the name of the Lord! Blessed is the coming kingdom of our ancestor David! Hosanna in the highest heaven!"	The whole multitude of the disciples began to praise God joyfully with a loud voice for all the deeds of power that they had seen, saying, "Blessed is the king who comes in the name of the Lord! Peace in heaven, and glory in the highest heaven!"

That last sentence of Luke's above recalls the conjunction of glory and peace in 2:14. Peace comes from heaven down to earth, but is always and ever a heavenly gift of God. That gift is further specified in the very next section, a unit found only in Luke:

As he came near and saw the city, he wept over it, saying, "If you, even you, had only recognized on this day
the things that make for peace! But now they are hidden
from your eyes. Indeed, the days will come upon you,
when your enemies will set up ramparts around you and
surround you, and hem you in on every side. They will
crush you to the ground, you and your children within
you, and they will not leave within you one stone upon
another; because you did not recognize the time of your
visitation from God. (19:41–44)

Luke is writing after the destruction of Jerusalem by the Roman legions in 70 CE. The peace of God did not come to Jerusalem (the city of peace) from Roman imperial violence, but
neither did it come from Jewish colonial rebellion.

There is an ironic comment on that in Acts. When Paul is
accused before the new governor Felix by the high-priestly
authorities in the later 50s, Luke has their lawyer Tertullus
say, "Your Excellency, because of you we have long enjoyed
peace" (24:2).

But how, then, does the peace of heaven descend to earth?
It can only come from nonviolent resistance. So, after Rome
has crucified Jesus and God has raised him, he returns to the
disciples, stands among them, and says to them, "Peace be
with you" (Luke 24:36).

Peace on Earth — But by What Means?

All of this raises one very clear question. In Matthew's Christmas story, Jesus is the Davidic Messiah who is the God-
appointed King of the Jews. But Herod is the Rome-appointed

King of the Jews. How exactly do those alternative kingdoms compare with one another? What is the essential difference between them—granted, of course, that any final answer must come not just from this overture, but only from the entire life story to follow?

The same question arises in Luke's Christmas story. Caesar Augustus brought "the whole world," as he claimed, under the peace of the Roman Empire—the Pax Romana, which was also the Pax Augustana. What, then, is this new peace announced as the good news of Jesus's birth as Savior, Messiah, and Lord? What is the content of this alternative—granted, once again, that any final answer must come not just from this overture, but only from the entire life story to follow?

How does Christ differ from Caesar? How does Roman imperial theology differ from early Christian theology? It will not do just to keep repeating claims without content or titles without interpretation—because they are the same for both sides.

Both proclaim that it started in heaven. For Augustus it was Jupiter's "good pleasure" in *Aeneid* 1.283 and for Jesus it was "God's favor" in Luke 2:14. In other words, both claim heavenly pleasure, favor, decision, and decree. Both visions announce the gospel of peace on earth and proclaim it as a new creation, a whole new start for the human race. And both link that gospel to the divine conception of a predestined savior.

Furthermore, both Roman imperial theology and early Christian theology assert the same titles for Augustus and for Jesus: Divine, Son of God, God, God from God, Lord, Redeemer Liberator, and Savior of the World. So, when you commit your life by faith to Augustus or to Jesus, and to Caesar or to Christ as their continuations, to what—precisely—do you pledge allegiance?

The Roman vision incarnated in the divine Augustus was peace through victory. The Christian vision incarnated in the divine Jesus was peace through justice. It is those alternatives that are at stake behind all the titles and countertitles, the claims and counterclaims.

Recall, from Chapter 3, that the viceroy for God's Great Cleanup of the World was to establish a world of nonviolence. But can that ever be done by violence—even by messianic, transcendental, angelic, or divine violence? Can it ever be done by the victory of a Great Final Battle or must it be done—if ever it is done—by the justice of a Great Final Feast?

The terrible truth is that our world has never established peace through victory. Victory establishes not peace, but lull. Thereafter, violence returns once again, and always worse than before. And it is that escalator violence that then endangers our world.

The four-week period of Advent before Christmas—and the six-week period of Lent before Easter—are times of penance and life change for Christians. In our book *The Last Week,* we suggested that Lent was a penance time for having been in the wrong procession and a preparation time for moving over to the right one by Palm Sunday. That day's violent procession of the horse-mounted Pilate and his soldiers was contrasted with the nonviolent procession of the donkey-mounted Jesus and his companions. We asked: in which procession would we have walked then and in which do we walk now?

We face a similar choice each Christmas, and so each Advent is a time of repentance for the past and change for the future. Do we think that peace on earth comes from Caesar or Christ? Do we think it comes through violent victory or nonviolent justice? Advent, like Lent, is about a choice of how to live personally and individually, nationally and internationally.

Christmas is not about tinsel and mistletoe or even ornaments and presents, but about what *means* will we use toward the *end* of a peace from heaven upon our earth. Or is "peace on earth" but a Christmas ornament taken each year from attic or basement and returned there as soon as possible?

PART III

LIGHT, FULFILLMENT, AND JOY

CHAPTER SEVEN

LIGHT AGAINST THE DARKNESS

The stories of the first Christmas are resplendent with light. In Matthew, the star of Bethlehem shines in the night sky to guide the wise men to the place of Jesus's birth. In Luke, the night is filled with light, radiant with the glory of the Lord, as angels bring the news of Jesus's birth to shepherds keeping watch over their flocks: "And the glory of the Lord shone all around them." And more, two of the hymns in Luke's story climax with light imagery: "The dawn from on high will break upon us, to give light to those who sit in darkness" (1:78–79); Jesus is "a light for revelation to the Gentiles and for glory to your people Israel" (2:32).

Later in this chapter, we will treat these texts in detail. But we begin with the symbolism of light and its meanings. Light is an ancient archetypal symbol. It is also central to ancient Judaism and early Christianity, the context in which Matthew and Luke wrote their stories of Jesus's birth.

And, to say the obvious, light in the darkness is central to the Christian celebration of Christmas. Jesus is born in the deepest darkness—in the middle of the night at the winter solstice. This is not historical time, not a historical fact about the date of Jesus's birth, but parabolic time, metaphorical time, sacred time, symbolic time. The symbolism is perfect.

Nobody knows the day, the month, or the season of the year of Jesus's birth. The date of December 25 was not decided upon until the middle of the 300s. Before then, Christians celebrated his birth at different times—including March, April, May, and November. But around the year 350 Pope Julius in Rome declared December 25 as the date, thereby integrating it with a Roman winter solstice festival celebrating the "Birthday of the Unconquered Sun." The Roman birthday of the sun became the Christian birthday of the Son.

To this association of the birth of Jesus with the winter solstice was added the symbolism of it happening at night. "Night" abounds in the words of familiar Christmas carols:

Silent night, holy night, all is calm, all is bright.

*O holy night, the stars are brightly shining; it is the night
    of our dear Savior's birth.*

*O little town of Bethlehem, how still we see thee lie.
Beneath thy deep and dreamless sleep, the silent stars roll by.
Yet in thy dark streets shineth the everlasting light.*

It came upon the midnight clear, that glorious song of old.

In the middle of the night, on the longest night of the year, the time of deepest darkness, Jesus is born. He is, as John 1:9 puts it, the true light that enlightens everyone, the light of the world.

LIGHT AS ARCHETYPAL SYMBOL

Light is an archetypal symbol. An archetype, as the roots of the word suggest, is an image, a "type" imprinted in human consciousness from ancient times, from "the beginning." Known across cultures, the archetype of light, with its opposite of darkness, is central to religious traditions around the world. It is also, as we will see, central to the Jewish Bible, the New Testament, and Roman imperial theology.

It is not difficult to understand why the symbolism of light is a universal archetype. We need only imagine how our ancestors experienced night and darkness. This requires some effort, for we need to imagine a time before we learned how to illumine and domesticate the night with artificial light. It was not so long ago. Only recently have cities been illumined at night; London was apparently the first, perhaps in the 1600s. It became common in cities only after the invention of gas lighting in the late 1700s. So also household lighting is recent. According to an exhibit entitled "The History of Light" at the Rijksmuseum in Amsterdam a few years ago, ordinary people—meaning the majority of the population—could not afford candles until around the year 1800. When night fell, it was dark, very dark. Our ancestors knew darkness in a way that we do not.

The archetypal associations, metaphorical associations, of night and darkness are many. In the dark, we cannot see, or at least not very well. Thus night and darkness are associated with blindness and limited vision. For the same reason, we easily get lost in the dark; we stumble around and cannot see our way. In the dark, we are often afraid. We do not know what might be going on: danger may lurk, spirits may roam, evil may be afoot. Night is the time when we are asleep, unconscious and unaware. Night and winter go together. The nights become longer, the earth loses its warmth and becomes cold and unfruitful. Darkness, grief, and mourning are associated. Grief is like a dark night, and mourners have worn dark clothing for centuries. So also night and death go together: the land of the dead is a place of great darkness.

No wonder our ancestors valued light, the day. They welcomed the dawn and celebrated the return of light at the winter solstice. No wonder religious traditions are filled with the language of light—of enlightenment, seeing, awakening, visions, and epiphanies. No wonder glory—which means radiance, luminosity—is a central quality of the sacred.

Given the above—we almost wrote, "in light of the above"—it is also no wonder that the associations of light and darkness are so rich in the Old Testament and earliest Christianity. Though this exposition of the significance of light imagery in the Old and New Testaments may at times seem like a detour, it is the main road for glimpsing what this archetypal image meant in the context of the world in which the birth stories originated.

LIGHT IN THE OLD TESTAMENT

Like the birth stories, the Old Testament is filled with the symbolism of light. In the story of creation with which the Bible of Jesus and early Christianity begins, light is the first of God's creative acts. On the first day of creation:

> God said, "Let there be light"; and there was light. And God saw that the light was good; and God separated the light from the darkness. God called the light Day, and the darkness he called Night. And there was evening and there was morning, the first day. (Gen. 1:3–5)

This light is not the light of the sun, moon, and stars; they are not created until the fourth day. Rather, the light of the first day of creation is primordial light, the light that existed before sun, moon, and stars.

In the stories of Israel's ancestors in the Pentateuch, light imagery often symbolizes the presence of God, the nearness of the sacred. For Abraham, the father of Israel, God's presence is imaged as "a smoking fire pot and a flaming torch" appearing to him "in a deep and terrifying darkness" (Gen. 15:12, 17). Abraham's grandson Jacob, the father of the twelve tribes of Israel, experiences in the night a fiery ladder with angels descending and ascending upon it and exclaims, "This is the gate of heaven" (Gen. 28:17). In the foundational story of the Pentateuch, the exodus from slavery in Egypt, Israel's ancestors are led by "a pillar of fire by night, to give them light" (Exod. 13:21).

Light imagery appears in a familiar line in one of the psalms: "Your word is a lamp to my feet and a light to my path" (Ps. 119:105). Here it is light as illumination—God's word is a lamp, lighting our way. In another psalm, the human yearning for the coming of dawn and the end of night becomes a metaphor for the psalmist's yearning for God:

> *I wait for the Lord, my soul waits, and in his word I hope;*
> *my soul waits for the Lord more than those who watch for the*
>   *morning,*
> *more than those who watch for the morning. (Ps. 130:5–6)*

The symbolism of light and darkness continues in the prophets. In the first part of the book of Isaiah, from the 700s BCE, the prophet associates the coming of light with the coming of the ideal king. The text begins: "The people who walked in darkness have seen a great light; those who lived in a land of deep darkness—on them has light shined" (9:2). As the passage continues, the "great light" shining "in a land of deep darkness" is the birth of the ideal king who would bring justice and peace. The words are familiar to millions because of Handel's *Messiah:*

> For a child has been born for us, a son given to us; authority rests upon his shoulders; and he is named Wonderful Counselor, Mighty God, Everlasting Father, Prince of Peace. His authority shall grow continually, and there shall be endless peace for the throne of David and his kingdom. He will establish it and uphold it with justice and with righteousness from this time onward and forevermore. The zeal of the Lord of hosts will do this. (Isa. 9:6–7)

This—the coming of the ideal king, the Prince of Peace who will uphold justice—is the coming of the light to those who live in a land of deep darkness.

In the last part of the book of Isaiah, from the 500s BCE, light symbolizes the glory of God, the radiant presence of God, and God's promise to Jerusalem. The words are addressed to the city, recently destroyed by the Babylonian conquest in 586 BCE and only humbly rebuilt after the Jewish return from exile in Babylon. Jerusalem has only a hint of its past glory as the home of Solomon's temple and the capital of a kingdom; those are gone. To Jerusalem stripped of its glory, the prophet promises God's glory, and the imagery is full of light:

> Arise, shine; for your light has come, and the glory of the Lord has risen upon you. For darkness shall cover the earth, and thick darkness the peoples; but the Lord will arise upon you, and his glory will appear over you. Nations shall come to your light, and kings to the brightness of your dawn. (Isa. 60:1–3)

Jerusalem, filled with the glory of God, will draw the nations to its light—kings will come to the brightness of its dawn. Here light is associated not only with God, but with God's dream for Jerusalem and the world.

Ancient Judaism also had a festival of light. Hanukkah was (and still is) an eight-day celebration of light as the winter solstice approaches. Originating in the second century BCE, it commemorates the rededication of the temple in Jerusalem after it had been desecrated by a foreign ruler. The rededication of the temple as the home of God's glory is celebrated as the darkness deepens.

LIGHT IN THE NEW TESTAMENT

The metaphorical richness of light—as God's presence and promise, God's illumination and God's dream—continues in earliest Christianity. Before turning to the birth stories, it is illuminating to see how central the imagery of light is in the rest of the New Testament. As we do so, our purpose is not to present a comprehensive study of all references to light in the New Testament. It is more modest and yet important: to illustrate the centrality of this archetypal metaphor in the multiple voices of early Christianity found in the New Testament. We begin with Paul.

Light Imagery in Paul's Letters

According to the book of Acts, Paul's life-transforming experience on the road to Damascus was an experience of the risen Christ as light. Acts tells the story three times (9:1–18; 22:6–16; 26:12–18). In the first telling, narrated in the third person, we are told, "Suddenly a light from heaven flashed around him"

(9:3). So also in the second telling, but now in first-person narration: "While I was on my way and approaching Damascus, about noon a great light from heaven suddenly shone about me" (22:6). The experience of the risen Christ as "a great light" initially blinded Paul, but three days later his sight was restored and "something like scales fell from his eyes" (9:18). Christ as "light" and the result as "seeing" are central in what may be the best-known conversion story in the world.

In his letters, Paul himself uses the imagery of light. In 2 Corinthians, he speaks of "the light of the gospel of the glory of Christ" (4:4) and then refers to the first act of creation:

> For it is the God who said, "Let light shine out of darkness," who has shone in our hearts to give the light of the knowledge of the glory of God in the face of Jesus Christ. (4:6)

The passage is rich and dense, and to suggest some of its possible meanings concisely risks not doing justice to it.

We begin by noting the obvious. It is filled with light imagery—not only the words "light," "darkness," "shine," and "shone," but also the word "glory." The biblical words translated into English as "the glory of God" have the connotation of a radiant, luminous presence. Glory, radiance, and luminosity go together. The glory of God is the radiant, luminous presence of God.

The passage piles up these images, as in "the *light* of the gospel of the *glory* of Christ." The gospel (not yet meaning a written document, but rather "the good news") is light, illumination. And it is "the gospel of the *glory* of Christ"—of the radiant presence of Christ, the luminosity of Christ. The gospel is light, and it is about light.

And the passage continues: this light, this glory, comes from "the God who said, 'Let light shine out of darkness.'" This God, the God who created light in the darkness, Paul says, "has shone in our hearts to give the light of the knowledge of the glory of God in the face of Jesus Christ." Here three images of light are piled together: God has "*shone* in our hearts, to give the *light* of the knowledge of the *glory* of God"—and all three are seen "in the face of Jesus Christ."

Though "face" is not a light metaphor, it is a visual metaphor. "In the face of Jesus Christ," we *see* "the light of the knowledge of the glory of God." It is an extraordinary and marvelous claim about Jesus: his "face" reveals the "light of the knowledge" that comes from the "glory of God." Further, he is the revelation of the God who said, "Let there be light." The God who created light in the beginning has now become known in Jesus. The light has become light in the face of Jesus.

Light Imagery in John's Gospel

Light and darkness are central to the presentation of Jesus in the gospel of John. Written near the end of the first century, John's gospel is a witness, a testimony, to how the Christian community for whom its author wrote saw Jesus. The imagery appears at the very beginning in the prologue to the gospel (1.1–18), much of which may have been an early Christian hymn or, at the very least, a prose poem.

John's prologue begins, as the book of Genesis does, with the words "In the beginning." And what was in the beginning was "the Word," *logos* in Greek. The Word, the *logos,* was not only with God in the beginning, but was God, and through the Word, the *logos,* God created everything that is. Then light imagery appears: "In the *logos* was life, and the life was *the light* of all people. The *light shines in the darkness,* and the darkness did not overcome it" (1:4–5). A few verses later: "The *true light,* which *enlightens* everyone, was coming into the world" (1:9). The light, of course, is Jesus.

Recall that John does not have a birth story. But this passage virtually functions at its equivalent: the coming of Jesus, the incarnation, is the coming of "the *true light,* which *enlightens* everyone." The imagery of light and darkness announced in the prologue continues throughout the gospel. For John, Jesus is "the light of the world" (8:12; 9:5).

Light Imagery in Revelation

To complete our illustrative survey of light imagery in the New Testament, we turn to the book of Revelation. This much misunderstood book concludes with a magnificent vision of the "new Jerusalem" (21:1–22:5). It is a vision of life on earth, for the "new Jerusalem" descends to the earth. In it there will be no more tears, no more mourning and crying and pain, and death will be no more (21:4). The city will be fantastically bejeweled and huge. It will have no temple, "for its temple is the Lord God the Almighty and the Lamb" (21:22).

Then the imagery turns to light:

And the city has no need of sun or moon to shine on it, for the glory of God is its light, and its lamp is the Lamb. The nations shall walk by its light, and the kings of the earth will bring their glory into it. Its gates will never be shut by day—and there will be no night there. (21:23–25)

A few verses later, the vision reaches its climax with a return to the theme of light: "And there will be no more night; they need no light of lamp or sun, for the Lord God will be their light" (22:5). The new Jerusalem is a city of light, and its light is the glory—the radiant presence—of God and Jesus.

All of the above—light imagery in the Old Testament and in early Christianity—is part of the context in which the stories of Jesus birth were told. Writing near the end of the first century, the authors of Matthew and Luke composed their gospels within the contexts of an early Christianity suffused with the imagery of light.

LIGHT IMAGERY IN MATTHEW'S STORY

Matthew uses the symbolism of light in his story of the star of Bethlehem that led the wise men to the place of Jesus's birth. The most widely known episode from Matthew's birth narrative and a centerpiece of Christmas pageants, it is part of the larger story of Herod who, like a new Pharaoh, seeks to kill the infant Jesus. As one born to be "King of the Jews," Jesus is a rival king in the conflict of kingships that runs through Matthew's story, which we treated in Chapter 6.

Here we focus on the use of light imagery in the story. In the relevant portions of Matthew 2:1–12, references to the star are italicized:

> In the time of King Herod, after Jesus was born in Bethlehem, wise men from the East came to Jerusalem, asking, "Where is the child who has been born King of the Jews? *For we have observed his star at its rising, and have come to pay him homage.*"
>
> Herod secretly called for the wise men and learned from them the exact time *when the star had appeared.*

Then he sent them to Bethlehem, saying, "Go and search diligently for the child; and when you have found him, bring me word so that I may also go and pay him homage." When they had heard the king, they set out; *and there, ahead of them, went the star that they had seen at its rising, until it stopped over the place where the child was. When they saw that the star had stopped, they were overwhelmed with joy.*

Virtually every year in the weeks before Christmas, stories appear in the media that seek to identify the star of Matthew's story with some natural phenomenon. The most common suggestions are a comet, a conjunction of planets, or a nova.

But attempts to identify the guiding star with a natural astronomical event are misguided. The star in Matthew's gospel does not simply shine in the sky; it moves. It not only leads the wise men westward to Jerusalem, but then turns and moves south to Bethlehem. There, *"it stopped over the place where the child was."* It leads the way to the place of Jesus's birth with the precision of a global positioning device. This is no comet or conjunction of planets or nova. The story of the star does not make a statement about an astronomical phenomenon, but a statement about Jesus: his birth is the coming of the light that draws wise men of the Gentiles to its radiance.

The Christian tradition has commonly spoken of three wise men and called them kings. Matthew, however, as mentioned earlier, does not say how many wise men there were or that they were kings. The notion that there were three comes from the three gifts they bring: gold, frankincense, and myrrh. Subsequent Christian tradition even gave the kings names: Caspar, Melchior, and Balthasar.

This notion that they were kings comes from an echo of a passage from Isaiah, one of the "light" texts cited earlier in this chapter. Recall that its opening words are addressed to postexilic Jerusalem: "Arise, shine; for your light has come, and the glory of the Lord has risen upon you. . . . Nations shall come to your light, and *kings* to the brightness of your dawn" (60:1, 3). Those who come to Jerusalem as the light are kings. Then gifts of gold and frankincense are mentioned: "They shall bring gold and frankincense, and shall proclaim the praise of the Lord" (60:6).

We do not know if Matthew had Isaiah 60 in mind when he wrote his story. Did he derive the notion of "the nations" coming to the light and two of the gifts (gold and frankincense) from this passage? Was he deliberately echoing Isaiah 60? What is clear is that later Christian tradition has elaborated Matthew's story by deriving the notion of kings from Isaiah 60.

What else can be said about the wise men, beyond the negative point that Matthew does not say they were three kings? Given that we do not think of the wise men as actual historical figures but as characters in a parabolic narrative, it may seem idle to speculate about who they were. But we can nevertheless ask who Matthew imagined them to be, just as we can ask such a question about characters in a parable.

They are *magi* (translated into English as "wise men"; the singular is *magus*), a word from which we get "magician." But they were not magicians in the modern sense of the word. Rather, the word refers to a kind of religious figure: *magi* had wisdom by being in touch with another reality. Their wisdom was a "secret wisdom," a kind not known by ordinary people. No doubt some were astrologers in the sense that they paid attention to "signs in the heavens," but to think of *magi* as primarily astrologers is misleading. Rather, *magi* were people with a more than earthly wisdom.

The *magi* in Matthew's story come "from the East." It is idle to speculate about what more specific geographical area they might have come from—this is sacred geography, not physical geography. What matters for Matthew is that they are *Gentiles*. As Gentiles, they are from "the nations." Wise men from the nations are drawn to the light of Jesus, kneel before him, and pay him homage. The nations acknowledge one born "King of the Jews"; he is their king as well.

The uses of light and darkness in this parabolic narrative are thus many and rich. Jesus's birth is the coming of light into the darkness. But the darkness seeks to extinguish the light (Herod's plot to kill Jesus). Drawn to the light, wise men from the nations pay homage to Jesus. Jesus is the light of the nations. Thus Matthew's story makes the point made in only slightly different language in John: "Jesus is the light of the world."

Of course, no concise set of sentences can capture all the meanings of this story. It cannot be reduced to statements. The narrative retains its evocative richness and metaphorical power. Like metaphorical narratives in general, it has a surplus of meaning. But we do think Matthew's story of the star of Bethlehem means at least as much as what we have suggested.

For a moment, we return to the truth of parable and the question of historical factuality. We do not think Matthew's story is historically factual. In our judgment, there was no special star, no wise men, and no plot by Herod to kill Jesus. So is the story factually true? No. But as parable, is it true? For us as Christians, the answer is a robust affirmative. Is Jesus light shining in the darkness? Yes. Do the Herods of this world seek to extinguish the light? Yes. Does Jesus still shine in the darkness? Yes.

LIGHT IMAGERY IN LUKE'S STORY

Before turning to the most familiar story that uses light imagery in Luke—angels singing in the night sky to shepherds as the glory of the Lord shone round about them—we treat Luke's use of the language of light in two of his hymns.

The Benedictus

The Benedictus, so named from its first word in the Latin version, is sung by Zechariah, the father of John the Baptizer. Struck dumb when he learns from an angel that he and his wife Elizabeth will conceive a son despite their advanced age, Zechariah regains his ability to speak after the birth and naming of John: "Immediately his mouth was opened and his tongue freed, and he began to speak, praising God" (1:64). His first words are the Benedictus, whose opening lines are familiar to millions of Christians:

> *Blessed be the Lord God of Israel,*
> *   for he has looked favorably on his people and redeemed*
> *   them.*
> *He has raised up a mighty savior for us*
> *   in the house of his servant David. (1:68–69)*

We begin with a comment about the word "savior." In the first century, it did not yet mean what it means for many Christians today. Because Christians have for centuries spoken of Jesus as saving us from our sins through his death on the cross, many Christians automatically connect Jesus as savior with atonement for sins. But in the Bible, the primary meaning of the term is "rescuer," "deliverer."

For example, Psalms speaks of God as Israel's "*Savior* who had done great things in Egypt . . . and awesome deeds by the Red Sea" (106:21–22). So also Hosea connects God as savior to the exodus: "Yet I have been the Lord your God ever since the land of Egypt; you know no God but me, and besides me there is no *savior*" (13:4). A song attributed to King David speaks of God as "my stronghold and my refuge, my *savior;* you save me from violence" (2 Sam. 22.3). Jeremiah addresses God as the "hope of Israel, its *savior* in time of trouble" (14:8). In none of these instances is there any connection between "savior" and being saved from sin. To think that speaking of Jesus as savior refers primarily to his death as a sacrifice for sin narrows and reduces the meaning of this rich term.

To return to the Benedictus: what the "mighty savior" of whom Zechariah sings will do is the theme of the middle part. He is the fulfillment of God's promise, "the oath that God swore to our ancestor Abraham," namely, "that we would be saved from our enemies and from the hand of all who hate us," so "that we, being rescued from the hands of our enemies, might serve God without fear, in holiness and righteousness before him all our days" (1:71, 73–75). "Being rescued from the hands of our enemies" is the role of the "mighty savior"; this is what it means to be saved.

Then, in the hymn's closing lines, light imagery appears. The lines are climax, not simply conclusion.

> *By the tender mercy of our God,*
>> *the dawn from on high will break upon us,*
> *to give light to those who sit in darkness and in the shadow*
>> *of death,*
>> *to guide our feet into the way of peace. (1:78–79)*

The passage echoes light and darkness texts from the Old Testament (Isa. 60:1–3; 42:6–7; Ps. 107:10). In archetypal and Jewish language, the coming of Jesus is "the dawn from on high" that gives "light to those who sit in darkness." The result is "to guide our feet into the way of peace." As we will see, the word "peace" appears in all three of Luke's passages about light.

The Nunc Dimittis

The Nunc Dimittis, sung by the aged Jewish prophet named Simeon in the temple as he holds the infant Jesus, is probably most well known by Christians, because of its frequent use in worship and devotion, in the words of the King James Version:

> *Lord, now lettest thou thy servant depart in peace,*
> *according to thy word;*
> *For mine eyes have seen thy salvation,*
> *which thou hast prepared before the face of all people,*
> *A light to lighten the Gentiles,*
> *and the glory of thy people Israel.* (2:29–32)

Simeon, Luke tells us, "was righteous and devout, looking forward to the consolation of Israel," and "it had been revealed to him by the Holy Spirit that he would not see death before he had seen the Lord's Messiah" (2:26). Now his desire has been fulfilled: he has seen God's salvation—and what Simeon has seen, of course, is Jesus. Jesus is God's salvation, that is, God's means of salvation.

The word "salvation," like the word "savior," has a meaning for many Christians much narrower than its biblical meaning. For many Christians, "salvation" is closely connected with postdeath existence, with "going to heaven." When the word is understood that way, Jesus as God's salvation becomes Jesus as God's means of "going to heaven." But in the Bible, the word has much more this-worldly, here-and-now meanings, including rescue, deliverance, liberation, protection, healing, and being made whole. Psalm 27:1 affirms: "The Lord is my light and my salvation; whom shall I fear? The Lord is the stronghold of my life; of whom shall I be afraid?"

Thus the meaning of "salvation" in the Nunc Dimittis is much the same as the meaning of "savior" in the Benedictus.

Simeon's song climaxes with light imagery, just as the Benedictus does. To return to the language of the NRSV, Jesus is "*a light for revelation to the Gentiles and for glory to your people Israel.*" Light and glory: light to the nations, glory to Israel. In different words, Simeon sings what Matthew says in his story of Jesus's birth: Jesus is the King of the Jews and light to the nations.

Glory in the Night Sky

We turn now to Luke's familiar story of angels appearing in the night to shepherds:

> In that region there were shepherds living in the fields, keeping watch over their flock by night. Then an angel of the Lord stood before them, and the glory of the Lord shone around them, and they were terrified. But the angel said to them, "Do not be afraid; for see—I am bringing you good news of great joy for all the people: to you is born this day in the city of David a Savior who is the Messiah, the Lord. This will be a sign for you: you will find a child wrapped in bands of cloth and lying in a manger." And suddenly there was with the angel a multitude of the heavenly host, praising God and saying,
>
> "*Glory to God in the highest heaven,*
> *And on earth peace among those whom he favors.*"
> (*2:8–14*)

The story is filled with light, radiance, luminosity, glory, revelation. As shepherds watch over their flock *by night,* an *angel* (a being of light) appears, and the *glory* of God *shines* around them. Then, after the angelic message is spoken, the night sky is filled with "a multitude of the heavenly host," the firmament ablaze with God's glory.

Whenever angels speak in the Bible, it is time to listen carefully. Their narrative function is to reveal the meaning of what is happening. To cite a classic example from the end of Luke's gospel, on Easter morning, angels say to the bewildered women at the tomb, "Why do you look for the living among the dead? He is not here, but has risen" (24:5). This is what the story of the empty tomb means.

So also in this story. The angel tells the shepherds what the display of God's glory in the night sky means. We italicize the terms that will receive the most comment.

> I am bringing you *good news* of great joy for all the people: to you is born this day in the city of David a *Savior* who is the *Messiah,* the *Lord.*

The words "Savior," "Messiah," and "Lord" are early and familiar Christian designations for Jesus. All have meanings within a Jewish context. "Savior," as noted above, has the primary meaning of "rescuer," "deliverer."

"Messiah" (synonymous with "Christ") in the Old Testament means "anointed one." By the first century, it commonly meant *the* anointed one promised by God, the hope of Israel. We saw in Chapter 3 that there was no unified messianic expectation in first-century Judaism, but a variety of expectations. But when the term "Messiah" was used, it was in the context of the one promised and anointed by God to be the rescuer of Israel (or, in the case of the Dead Sea community, "ones"—they expected two messiahs). In the New Testament, it is one of the most common designations of Jesus, as in the phrase "Jesus Christ." The phrase means "Jesus the Messiah," the one promised and anointed by God.

In the Septuagint, the Greek translation of the Old Testament (the version of the Bible most widely known by early Christians), *kyrios* (Greek for "Lord") is often used to translate the Hebrew word for "God." "Lord" thus had connotations of divinity: God was *kyrios*. It also could mean "master," in the sense of somebody to whom one is in a relationship of allegiance, commitment, or loyalty. In the New Testament, "Jesus is Lord" is perhaps the most common post-Easter affirmation about him. Importantly, it combines both connotations of the word "Lord": divine status and our allegiance. Lordship and loyalty go together.

Thus the angelic message expresses central Christian convictions about Jesus. It is the gospel in miniature. Indeed, the angel actually uses the Greek word for "gospel" (or "good news"): Jesus is Savior, Messiah, and Lord. All have rich meanings within the framework of their Jewish roots. But the angelic message has a second framework of meaning as well; namely, its language echoes and counters Roman imperial theology.

We have already noted that Roman imperial theology regularly spoke of the emperor as "Lord," "Son of God," and sometimes as "Savior." Moreover, as we saw in Chapter 6, the birth of the greatest emperor, Caesar Augustus, was "gospel," "good news," for the whole world. Imperial theology had its gospel, and early Christianity had its gospel.

The counterpointing of imperial theology goes further. Light is also central to imperial theology. We see this clearly in the stories of the birth of Augustus (born Octavian). Conceived by the god Apollo in his human mother, Atia, he was "Son of God" by Apollo—and Apollo was the god of light (as well as order and reason). Moreover, on the night of his conception, Atia's husband, Octavius, had a dream in which he saw the sun rising from his wife's womb. Caesar Augustus as son of the god Apollo was the coming of light to the world. But, according to Luke (and Matthew and John), *Jesus* is the light in the darkness. The other one claimed to be light in the darkness is not. Indeed, *that light* is darkness.

There is one more counterpoint to imperial theology. After the angel in a blaze of light announces to the shepherds the "good news" that "a Savior, who is the Messiah, the Lord" has been born for them, an angelic chorus filling the night sky breaks into song:

> *Glory to God in the highest heaven,*
>   *and on earth peace among those whom he favors. (2:14–15)*

We already discussed that closing phrase, "among those whom [God] favors," in Chapter 6. Here we emphasize the phrase "on earth peace," or, more commonly, "peace on earth." As in Luke's use of light imagery in the hymns, the word "peace" again appears.

Within Roman imperial theology, as we saw in Chapters 3 and 6, the emperor was the one who had brought peace on earth. In one sense, Augustus had: he brought an end to the civil war that had wracked the Roman world for decades. There was Pax Romana, "the peace of Rome."

Of course, the peace of Rome did not mean the end of war. Wars to conquer additional territory and wars to suppress insurrections continued. From the vantage point of the conquered and oppressed, imperial peace looked very different.

The Roman historian Tacitus, for example, placed the following speech on the lips of the Scottish general Calgacus as he prepared his doomed troops for battle with the legions of the Roman general Agricola in the later 70s or early 80s CE:

Robbers of the world, now that earth fails their all-dev-astating hands, they probe even the sea: if their enemy have wealth, they have greed; if he be poor, they are am-bitious; East nor West has glutted them; alone of man-kind they covet with the same passion want [poor lands] as much as wealth [rich lands]. To plunder, butcher, steal, these things they misname empire: they make a desert and they call it peace. (*Agricola* 30; brackets ours)

This is how many experienced the Pax Romana: "they make a desert and they call it peace." But Rome and its emperors saw themselves as having brought "peace on earth."

The song of the angels proclaims a different source and kind of peace. Jesus—as Savior, Messiah, and Lord—is the one who brings peace on earth. This is the peace of the king-dom of God, a peace based upon justice. The peace of empire is based on oppression and violence. Just as Matthew tells the story of Jesus's birth as a conflict between two kingships, so Luke tells the story of his birth as a conflict between two dif-ferent kinds of peace. There is the "good news" of empire and the "good news" of Jesus.

The angelic revelation comes to shepherds. Tourists and pilgrims to Bethlehem today are commonly shown not only the Church of the Nativity, but "Shepherds Field," where the angels appeared to them. These are sacred sites, even as they are not historical. And within the parabolic narrative of the birth stories, shepherds have a particular significance.

Shepherds were from the marginalized peasant class, the class that most acutely experienced oppression and exploitation by Rome and her client rulers. They were therefore among the "lowly" and "hungry" of Mary's Magnificat hymn in Luke 1:52–53. Their occupation may also recall David "keeping the sheep" of his father Jesse (1 Sam. 16:11) and protecting them (1 Sam. 17:15–36).

That they are the first ones to hear of Jesus's birth is significant: the good news comes to the poor and despised. It is consistent with the portrait of Jesus in the gospels. Matthew, Mark, and Luke all report that Jesus's message and activity were directed primarily to the peasant class. According to them, the only city that Jesus ever went to was Jerusalem. Otherwise, he was active in the countryside, in small towns and villages where the peasant population lived. As Luke later puts it, Jesus's message was "good news to the poor," "release to the captives," "sight to the blind," and "to let the oppressed go free" (4:18). The message to the shepherds foreshadows the message of Jesus.

ROME: APOLLO OR PYTHON?

This book is based on the birth stories of Jesus in Matthew 1–2 and Luke 1–2, and we usually think of them as the only two such narratives in the New Testament. But there is actually a third one, an absolutely fascinating mythological one, and one that serves to consummate their anti-imperial thrust.

This third birth story of Jesus has a dragon in it. It is found in the book of Revelation (also known as the Apocalypse), written near the end of the first century by an early Christian known as John of Patmos (Patmos is an island off the coast of Asia Minor). Like the stories in Matthew and Luke, it uses imagery associated with light and darkness to challenge Rome's claim to be the light of the world.

In Revelation 12, one of John's visions describes a woman about to give birth to a child "who is to rule all the nations." But a dragon waits to devour the child. In the symbolic and mythological language that abounds in Revelation, which is often interpreted without regard to its late first-century matrix:

> A great portent appeared in heaven: a woman clothed with the sun, with the moon under her feet, and on her head a crown of twelve stars. She was pregnant and was crying out in birth pangs, in the agony of giving birth. Then another portent appeared in heaven: a great red dragon, with seven heads and ten horns. . . . The dragon stood before the woman who was about to bear a child, so that he might devour her child as soon as it was born. And she gave birth to a son, a male child, who is to rule all the nations with a rod of iron. But her child was snatched away and taken to God and his throne. (12:1–5)

Later the dragon is called "the ancient serpent" (12:9) and "a beast rising out of the sea" (13:1).

It is clear that the child is Jesus, and the dragon, the ancient serpent, the beast, is Rome, the incarnation of empire of that time. After the dragon, the beast, the ancient serpent, loses a battle in heaven, he is cast down to the earth, where he rules the world. Later in Revelation, we are told that the beast is the city built on seven hills that rules the world (17:9, 18). In the first century, that could only mean Rome.

Moreover, we are told the "number" of the beast: "Its number is six hundred sixty-six" (13:18). Using an ancient Jewish technique for encoding a name into a number, called *gematria,* the number 666 decodes into "Caesar Nero," the emperor Nero. Nero ruled the empire from 54 to 69 CE and was the first emperor to actively persecute the followers of Jesus. According to early Christian tradition, both Peter and Paul were executed during Nero's reign.

John's vision directly challenges Roman imperial theology. His vision of a woman about to give birth while a great serpent waits to devour the child mimics and subverts the story of the birth of Apollo. Recall that Apollo, the god of light (and reason and order) was the father of Caesar Augustus. Augustus was "Son of God" by Apollo—and Apollo in turn was "Son of God" by Zeus, the supreme god of the Roman and Greek pantheon.

The story of Apollo's birth is narrated in the myth of Apollo and Python. Apollo was conceived by Zeus in his human mother, Leto (or Leda). As she was about to give birth to Apollo, a serpentine monster named Python waited to devour him. Though we use the word "python" to refer to a particular species of large snake, Python in this story is a mythical creature, the primeval monster, the ancient serpent, the primordial dragon, the source of evil and chaos. But Zeus comes to the rescue of Leto and Apollo, snatches them up from Python's menace, and carries them to a place of safety. After Apollo has grown up, he slays Python, bringing light, order, and reason to the world. Apollo, god of light, triumphs over primordial chaos.

The author of Revelation knows and echoes this story, but applies it to Jesus. It is a magnificent reversal, a stunning subversion, of imperial theology. Rome and its emperor are not Apollo, the bringer of light, but Python, the primordial serpent that seeks to destroy the light and to throw the world into monstrous chaos. Augustus was the son of Apollo, as were his successors. Indeed, Nero—whose name is 666—sometimes even dressed as Apollo. But, the author of Revelation asserts, Jesus is the true light of the world. Jesus is Apollo—Rome and its emperor are not. Rome, empire, is Python, the beast.

Thus Matthew and Luke and Revelation make rich use of the archetypal imagery of light. As in the Old Testament, light is associated with the presence of God and God's glory. Light in the darkness is about illumination and seeing. It includes seeing that imperial theology legitimates darkness and the rule of "the beast." And light is associated with salvation—about the coming of God's ideal world, of God's dream for the earth.

LIGHT: PERSONAL AND POLITICAL

The imagery of light in the darkness has been central to the Christian tradition since its beginning. Ancient Christian prayers as evening falls sound the theme again and again:

Light and peace, in Jesus Christ our Lord.

Jesus said, "You are the light of the world. A city built on a hill cannot be hid. No one lights a lamp to put it under a bucket, but on a lampstand where it gives light for everyone. . . . And you, like the lamp, must shed light among all people."

For the same God who said, "Out of darkness let light shine," has caused his light to shine within us, to give the light of revelation—the revelation of the glory of God in the face of Jesus Christ.

Almighty God, we give you thanks for surrounding us, as daylight fades, with the brightness of the vesper light; and we implore you of your great mercy that, as you enfold us with the radiance of this light, so you would shine into our hearts the brightness of your Holy Spirit.

Dispel the darkness of our hearts, that by your brightness
we may know you to be the true God and eternal light.

Be our light in the darkness, O Lord, and in your great
mercy defend us from all perils and dangers of this night.

O gracious light, pure brightness of the ever-living God in
heaven, O Jesus Christ, holy and blessed.

Like much of the Bible's language, the imagery of light is
both personal and political. The contrasts between darkness
and light are correlated with other central contrasts: bondage and liberation, exile and return, injustice and justice, violence and peace, falsehood and truth, death and life. These
contrasts all have a personal meaning as well as a political
meaning. It is important to see both. So it is with the stories of
Jesus's birth. They address our personal yearning and the politics of his world and ours. To see only the personal meaning is
to miss half of their meaning.

CHAPTER EIGHT

JESUS AS THE FULFILLMENT OF PROPHECY

The fulfillment of prophecy is a major theme of the Christmas stories in Matthew and Luke. Both emphasize that Jesus is the fulfillment of God's promises to Israel and the consummation of its longing.

To some degree, we have already treated in earlier chapters how Matthew and Luke use the Old Testament. Recall how the story of Pharaoh and Moses shaped Matthew's story of Herod and Jesus; how both Matthew and Luke proclaim that Jesus is the completion of the Law and the Prophets, not their replacement; and how both use light symbolism from the Old Testament in their testimony to the significance of the birth of Jesus.

In this chapter we focus on how Matthew and Luke sound the theme of fulfillment as they use texts from the Old Testament in their stories of Jesus's nativity. They do so in very different ways.

MATTHEW AND THE OLD TESTAMENT

Matthew's testimony to Jesus as the fulfillment of prophecy treats specific texts from the Old Testament as if they were predictions of Jesus. He uses what is commonly called a "prediction-fulfillment formula." With minor variations, the gist of the formula is *"Then was fulfilled what had been spoken by the prophet,"* followed by a passage from the Old Testament. This is a characteristic of Matthew as an author in his gospel as a whole. He directly quotes the Old Testament forty times. Thirteen or fourteen times (scholars differ on the number), he uses the prediction-fulfillment formula cited above.

In his Christmas story, he does so five times. We list them here together; later we will comment on each.

Following the story of an angel telling Joseph that Mary's pregnancy is from the Holy Spirit: *"All this took place to fulfill what had been spoken by the Lord through the prophet:* 'Look, the virgin shall conceive and bear a son, and they shall name him Emmanuel, which means "God is with us."'" (1:22–23)

In the context of scribes telling Herod the Great where the Messiah was to be born: *"For so it has been written by the prophet:* 'And you, Bethlehem, in the land of Judah, are by no means least among the rulers of Judah; for from you shall come a ruler who is to shepherd my people Israel.'" (2:5–6)

In the context of the holy family's return from Egypt after they had fled there to escape Herod's plot to kill Jesus: *"This was to fulfill what had been spoken by the Lord through the prophet,* 'Out of Egypt I have called my son.'" (2:15)

Following Herod's slaughter of children under two in and around Bethlehem: *"Then was fulfilled what had been spoken through the prophet Jeremiah:* 'A voice was heard in Ramah, wailing and loud lamentation, Rachel weeping for her children; she refused to be consoled, because they are no more.'" (2:17–18)

Following the move to Nazareth of Jesus and his family: "There he made his home in a town called Nazareth, *so that what had been spoken through the prophets might be fulfilled,* 'He will be called a Nazorean.'" (2:23)

Before we analyze these texts, we note the effect of Matthew's use of the Old Testament on the understanding of the relationship of Old Testament prophecy to Jesus. Through the centuries, most Christians have extended, consciously or unconsciously, Matthew's use to their hearing of Old Testament citations in the New Testament as a whole. It became a paradigm, a way of seeing, the relationship between the Old Testament and the New Testament.

It led to the notion that the Old Testament predicts not only the birth of Jesus with detailed specificity, but also his life, death, and resurrection. It created the notion that there was a collection of "messianic prophecies" in the time of Jesus. These, along with their fulfillment in the New Testament, are listed in Bible handbooks widely read by Protestant Christians a half century ago and still used in conservative Christian circles today. It is the basis for what is sometimes called "the argument from prophecy"; namely, the fulfillment of prophecy *proves* that Jesus is the Messiah, the promised one of Israel.

It has also led to a negative attitude toward "the Jews." How could the Jewish people fail to recognize Jesus as their Messiah, despite the clarity and precision with which he had been predicted? From this point of view, only darkened minds (or even willful blindness) could fail to see how exactly Jesus fulfilled the Old Testament. It has contributed, sometimes unconsciously, to Christian anti-Semitism, just as, at the other end of Jesus's life, a common reading of the stories of his crucifixion has contributed to Christian disparagement of "the Jews" because "they rejected their own Messiah."

The author of Matthew perhaps bears some responsibility for this, even though he could not have known how his words would be heard and used by Christians centuries later. Even more, what is responsible for this way of seeing his use of the Old Testament is a historically uninformed reading of his Christmas story. We turn now to the light that a historically informed reading sheds.

They Are Not Predictions

We begin with the foundational claim of a historical approach to Matthew's use of the Old Testament. In their historical contexts in the Old Testament, *none of the five passages is a prediction of the distant future or a prediction of Jesus*. Because this claim is crucial for seeing what is going on in Matthew, we illustrate it in each case. We warn readers that our exposition will seem negative for the next few pages, as if we are discrediting Matthew. But the result is, we are convinced, a richer understanding of these passages.

Virgin Birth Predicted? Matthew's first prediction-fulfillment formula cites Isaiah 7.14 to comment on Jesus's conception and naming: "All this took place to fulfill what had been spoken by the Lord through the prophet: '"Look, the virgin shall conceive and bear a son, and they shall name him 'Emmanuel,' which means 'God is with us.'"

Yet in its context in Isaiah, it is not a prediction of an event far in the future. The fuller context is Isaiah 7:10–16. Rather than printing the passage in full, we summarize it, even as we encourage readers to read it themselves. The words are addressed to King Ahaz, ruler of the southern kingdom of Judah in the eighth century BCE. The kings of two neighboring countries have surrounded Jerusalem with their armies in order to conquer it and replace Ahaz with a king more to their liking.

Ahaz, of course, is frightened. But Isaiah promises Ahaz a sign from God that he and his kingdom will be delivered. The sign will be the naming of a child soon to be born. This is the context for 7:14. It reads slightly differently in Isaiah from the way Matthew quotes it:

> The Lord himself will give you a sign. Look, the young woman is with child and shall bear a son, and shall name him Immanuel.

In Hebrew, the name to be given to the child, Immanuel, is not a proper name, but a phrase. As already noted, it means "God is with us." This will be the sign to King Ahaz: the symbolic naming of a child who is about to be born.

The symbolic naming of a child with a phrase that conveys a message occurs elsewhere in the prophets. Isaiah mentions two others: in 7:3, a child named Shear-jashub, which means

"A remnant shall return"; and in 8:3, Maher-shalal-hash-baz, which means "The spoil speeds, the prey hastens." Hosea also gave symbolic names to children. Lo-ruhamah means "Not pitied" (1:6) and was a sign that God would not show compassion upon an Israel that had grown radically unjust and idolatrous. Another child was named Lo-ammi, "Not my people" (1:8), meaning that the Israelite kingdom of the eighth century BCE would no longer be God's people.

To return to the Isaiah text, the sign is the naming of the child, "God is with us." The meaning of the naming in its historical context of the eighth century BCE is clear: Isaiah proclaimed that God would be with Ahaz and the people of Jerusalem in their present crisis.

The rest of the fuller context supports this reading. The two verses immediately following Isaiah 7:14 locate the meaning of the sign in its present and immediate future:

> He [Immanuel] shall eat curds and honey by the time he knows how to refuse the evil and choose the good. For before the child knows how to refuse the evil and choose the good, the land before whose two kings you are in dread will be deserted. (7:15–16)

By the time this child named "God is with us" is old enough to know the difference between right and wrong, the siege of the city would be lifted and the crisis Ahaz was facing would be over.

Two differences between wording of the text in Isaiah and Matthew's citation are worth noting. First, the Hebrew text of Isaiah 7:14 uses the word for "young woman." It says nothing about virginity. Of course, if she were unmarried, her virginity could virtually be taken for granted in that culture. People didn't date. But the text doesn't say that she was unmarried; the natural assumption is that she was a young married woman who would soon give birth. Matthew, however, uses the Greek word for "virgin." So does the early translation of the Hebrew Old Testament into Greek known as the Septuagint, the one most widely known by early Christians. Most likely, Matthew was using the Septuagint.

The issue of whether to translate Isaiah 7:14 as referring to a virgin or to a young woman has caused controversy among Christians. Until recently, most English translations of the verse used the word "virgin," thus conforming it to Matthew's use. Then, just over fifty years ago, the Revised Standard Version of the Bible (RSV) correctly translated the Hebrew word in Isaiah 7:14 as "young woman." Some Christians reacted strongly, alleging that the translators of the RSV were denying the virgin birth of Jesus by denying that it was predicted in prophecy. In a few places, Christians even burned copies of the RSV.

The second difference between Isaiah 7:14 and Matthew's citation of it is that, in Isaiah, the young woman is *already* with child, already pregnant. This points us back once again to the meaning of these words in their own time in the eighth century BCE. The sign in Isaiah concerns not how the child would be conceived, but the naming of the child. Isaiah 7:14 is not a prediction of a miraculous birth centuries later, not a prediction of Jesus.

Birth in Bethlehem Predicted? Matthew's second use of the formula is spoken by scribes in the court of King Herod. When Herod inquires of them where the Messiah will be born, they reply:

In Bethlehem of Judea. For so it has been written by the prophet: "And you, Bethlehem, in the land of Judah, are

by no means least among the rulers of Judah; for from
you shall come a ruler who is to shepherd my people
Israel."

This is the only one of Matthew's formula citations that, in its
Old Testament context, refers to an indefinite future.

The words are mostly from Micah, with a small portion
of 2 Samuel added. Micah 5:2 expresses the hope for an ideal
king who will come from Bethlehem:

But you, O Bethlehem of Ephrathah, who are one of the
little clans of Judah, from you shall come forth for me
one who is to rule in Israel, whose origin is from of old,
from ancient days.

The image of the ideal king as "a ruler who is to shepherd my
people Israel" comes from 2 Samuel 5:2, a promise given to
David:

It is you who shall be shepherd of my people Israel, you
who shall be ruler over Israel.

And, as you will recall from Chapter 6, David was the literal
shepherd of his father's sheep before he became the metaphorical shepherd of his God's people.

The shepherd image is also found in Micah. As the Micah
passage continues, it speaks of what the ideal king will be
like:

He shall stand and feed his flock in the strength of the
Lord, in the majesty of the name of the Lord his God.
And they shall live secure, for now he shall be great to
the ends of the earth; and he shall be the one of peace.
(5:4–5)

Is Matthew's use of this combined text from Micah and 2 Samuel a *prediction* of the place of Jesus's birth, namely, Bethlehem? No. Rather, it is ancient Israel's yearning for a king like David, the great king, the shepherd king. Under the kingship of one like David, "they shall live secure," for "he shall be the one of peace." It is hope and promise, not prediction.

Indeed, rather than being a prediction of the place of Jesus's birth, the passage from Micah is seen by most mainstream scholars as the reason for the Christmas stories narration that he was born in Bethlehem. He was probably born in Nazareth, as the common appellation "Jesus of Nazareth" suggests. Birth in Bethlehem is a claim in symbolic language that he is the "son of David," the ideal king.

Flight to Egypt and Return? Matthew's third use of the formula occurs in the context of Joseph, Mary, and Jesus's fleeing to Egypt to escape Herod's plot to kill Jesus. After Herod dies, the family returns to their homeland. "This," Matthew says, "was to fulfill what had been spoken by the Lord through the prophet, 'Out of Egypt I have called my son.'"

The citation is from Hosea, who spoke in the eighth century BCE. It was not a prediction. In Hosea 11:1, as its fuller context makes clear, the reference is to a past event (the exodus from Egypt), not a prediction of the future. The fuller context is, with the words that Matthew cites in italics:

When Israel was a child, I loved him, and *out of Egypt I called my son.* The more I called them, the more they went from me; they kept sacrificing to the Baals, and offering incense to idols. Yet it was I who taught Ephraim [another name for Israel] to walk, I took them up in my arms; but they did not know that I healed them. I led

them with cords of human kindness, with bands of love.
I was to them like those who lift infants to their cheeks. I
bent down to them and fed them. (Hos. 11:1–4)

Looking back to the time of the exodus and wilderness experience, Hosea speaks of God's love for Israel in its infancy,
Israel as God's "child," as God's "son." God led the Israelites
with "cords of kindness" and "bands of love," taught them how
to walk, healed them, fed them, like parents "who lift infants
to their cheeks." God's tender care in the past is contrasted to
their faithlessness in the present. This is reminiscence about
the past and indictment of the present, not prediction of the
future.

Lamentation of the Mothers of Bethlehem? The fourth citation, from Jeremiah 31:15, follows Herod's killing of all the
children in and around Bethlehem who were two years old or
under. This, Matthew writes, "fulfilled what had been spoken
through the prophet Jeremiah: 'A voice was heard in Ramah,
wailing and loud lamentation, Rachel weeping for her children; she refused to be consoled, because they are no more.'"

Once again, this is not prediction. Rachel was one of the
mothers of Israel and the favorite wife of Jacob, the father of
the twelve tribes. By the time of Jeremiah in the late seventh
and early sixth centuries BCE, she was a figure of the distant
past, having lived, according to Genesis, before the time of the
exodus. Rachel "weeping for her children" with "wailing and
loud lamentation" is a personification of the mother of Israel
grieving the death and deportation of her children, the Israelites, at the hands of either the Assyrian Empire in the eighth
century BCE or the Babylonian Empire in the early sixth century BCE.

Home in Nazareth Predicted? Matthew's fifth use of the formula occurs at the very end of his Christmas story. The holy family has now returned to the Jewish homeland from Egypt, but instead of going back to Bethlehem (their home in Matthew), they move to Nazareth. This, Matthew says, took place "so that what had been spoken through the prophets might be fulfilled, 'He will be called a Nazorean.'" This citation can he treated very concisely, for there is no such passage in the Old Testament, though there have been many scholarly speculations about what Matthew may have had in mind. Perhaps, as we suggested in Chapter 2, Matthew created this fifth prophetic fulfillment in order to satisfy his fondness for patterns of five, even though he had to invent a "prediction" to do so.

More Reflections on Matthew's Use of the Old Testament

Broadly speaking, there are three very different ways of seeing what Matthew is doing with his use of the prediction-fulfillment formula. The first, affirmed by fundamentalist and many conservative-evangelical Christians, defends what Matthew has done. It argues that these passages from the Old Testament are messianic prophecies and thus predictions of Jesus's birth and life, in spite of the fact that they were not understood as such in their ancient Jewish context. This view is grounded in the notion of biblical infallibility and inerrancy: if the Bible (in this case, Matthew) says these were predictions, then they are predictions.

The apparent discrepancy between their meaning in the Old Testament and their meaning in Matthew is explained by affirming that some prophetic passages have *a double meaning*—a meaning for their own time (the time of Isaiah, Hosea,

Jeremiah, and so forth) and a second and fuller meaning as disclosed by their use in the New Testament. Thus the prophets were saying more than they knew. But this also means that nobody thought of these as predictions until after they were "fulfilled."

The second way of seeing Matthew's use of the fulfillment formula is the polar opposite of the above. It does not defend what Matthew has done, but discredits him. It sees Matthew as taking these passages out of their ancient contexts and making them mean something they didn't intend to mean in order to prove that Jesus was the Messiah. He twisted the Old Testament to make his point. It sees the whole process as illegitimate and its results unworthy of being taken seriously. Occasionally, the discrediting of what Matthew has done becomes part of a larger "debunking" of the gospels and the Bible as a whole. If Matthew has done this, how can we trust anything else the gospels and the Bible say?

Note that both those who defend what Matthew has done and those who discredit it share in common the view that Matthew intended the passages he cites to be understood as *predictions* of the Messiah *fulfilled* in Jesus, thereby *proving* that he is the promised one of Israel, Messiah, and Son of God. They differ about whether Matthew has done this convincingly; the first say yes, the second no.

There is a third way of seeing Matthew's use of the fulfillment formula, and this is how we see it. We agree with the second view that the Old Testament passages cited by Matthew were not predictions. But we do not assume that Matthew thought they were. Moreover, we do not assume that Matthew was trying to prove that Jesus was the Messiah. We (and scholars in general) believe that Matthew was writing for "insiders," for his own Christian Jewish community, for Jews who already believed that Jesus was the Messiah. His exposition was not meant to convince "outsiders," but to express the convictions of "insiders."

Within this third way of seeing, Matthew's use of the Old Testament is testimony, witness, and conviction. For Matthew and his community, Jesus was the Messiah. As such, he was the fulfillment of God's promise and Israel's yearning. To express this, Matthew "mined" the Old Testament, the sacred scripture of his community, for passages that he could integrate into his narrative, seeing the story of Jesus "prefigured" there.

In this, he was like other authors in the ancient Mediterranean world. Roman and Greek writers, for example, regularly "mined" Homer, finding events in their time "prefigured" in the ancient texts. As mentioned in an earlier chapter, Homer's *Iliad* and *Odyssey* prefigured Virgil's *Aeneid,* and Aeneas himself prefigured Augustus. Virgil's Augustus as the Trojan Caesar and Matthew's Jesus as the Davidic Messiah prove nothing, but explain everything. This is the use of ancient language to express present conviction.

Thus we do not understand Matthew's use of the Old Testament as an attempt to *prove* that Jesus was the Messiah. Rather, it is testimony to his and his community's way of seeing Jesus, and seeing him in relationship to the ancient scriptures of their Jewish tradition. It expresses their conviction that he not only stood in continuity with them, but was the culmination of them.

Moreover, in most of Matthew's citations of the Old Testament, it is not "the miracle of prediction" that is emphasized, but an affirmation about who Jesus had become in the experience and thought of his community. "Out of Egypt I have called my son" affirms that Jesus is God's Son and that he relived the exodus, the great formative event of Israel's history. Jesus is the true "King of the Jews," the one promised in the book of Micah, the ruler born in Bethlehem "who is to shepherd my people Israel" and be a king of peace.

Even his use of Isaiah 7:14 in his story of Mary's virginal conception seems more focused on Jesus as Emmanuel, "God is with us," than on the miracle of conception. Matthew not only uses the Emmanuel theme in his Christmas story, but returns to it at the very end of his gospel. The last words of his gospel, which are also the last words of the risen Christ to his followers, are, "*I am with you* always, to the end of the age" (28.20). The one born Emmanuel is now the one who says, "I am with you always." For Matthew, Jesus is Emmanuel, both as a figure of history and as the risen Christ. This is New Testament testimony, not Old Testament prediction. In this sense, Jesus fulfills God's promise and Israel's yearning for Emmanuel, for the abiding presence of God with us.

Luke and the Old Testament

Luke uses the Old Testament very differently in his Christmas story. He does not use a prediction-fulfillment formula. Indeed, he does not even quote a verse from the Old Testament. He does, however, proclaim the continuity of Jesus with Israel and his fulfillment of God's promise to Israel in more than one way.

We see the theme of fulfillment with great clarity in the songs of Mary, Zechariah, and Simeon, the canticles known by millions of Christians as the Magnificat, the Benedictus, and the Nunc Dimittis. Although most scholars think of these as ancient Christian hymns, perhaps we should think of them as "chants"—hymns sung repetitively.

As early Christian hymns, they are neither reports about what Mary and Zechariah and Simeon said nor Luke's free creations. Rather, they are pre-Lukan Christian canticles. Though our focus is on how Luke uses them, it is intriguing to think that we are hearing "pregospel" Christian communities at worship in these texts. This is what the gospel, "the good news," of Jesus meant to them. And by including these in his Christmas story Luke affirms that this is what the gospel of Jesus meant to him.

Both the tone and the specific language of these hymns express the theme of fulfillment. The tone is jubilant, ringing with the conviction that God's promises are being fulfilled. Consider the opening words of each:

> *Magnificat:* "My soul magnifies the Lord, and my spirit rejoices in God my Savior, for he has looked with favor on the lowliness of his servant."

> *Benedictus:* "Blessed be the Lord God of Israel, for he has looked favorably on his people and redeemed them. He has raised up a mighty savior for us."

> *Nunc Dimittis:* "Master, now you are dismissing your servant in peace, according to your word; for my eyes have seen your salvation."

So also the language of these hymns sounds the theme of fulfillment. Rather than quoting verses from the Old Testament as Matthew does, Luke echoes phrases from ancient Israel's scriptures. He does so again and again.

Because it might be tedious as well as unnecessary to treat the echoes of Old Testament language in all three hymns, we focus on the Magnificat, sung by Mary. The Magnificat as a whole echoes the form of an Old Testament hymn of praise, a psalm of thanksgiving. Scholars agree that it is modeled on a hymn attributed to Hannah, the mother of the prophet Samuel some thousand years earlier. Hannah was one of the barren women in the Old Testament to whom God granted a child through a divinely bestowed conception.

The opening line of the Magnificat, given above, echoes the opening line of Hannah's hymn in 1 Samuel 2:1: "My heart exults in the Lord; my strength is exalted in my God." And, though Hannah's song is the model, it also echoes phrases from other Old Testament passages:

> Then my soul shall rejoice in the Lord, exulting in his deliverance. (Ps. 35:9)

> Yet I will rejoice in the Lord; I will exult in the God of my salvation. (Hab. 3:18)

> If only you will look on the misery of your servant. (1 Sam. 1:11)

The next few lines of the Magnificat echo language from the Psalms. "His mercy is for those who fear him from generation to generation" is similar to Psalm 103:17: "The steadfast love of the Lord is from everlasting to everlasting on those who fear him." Then, "He has shown strength with his arm; he has scattered the proud in the thoughts of their hearts" resembles Psalm 89:10: "You scattered your enemies with your mighty arm."

The closing lines of the Magnificat, "He has helped his servant Israel, in remembrance of his mercy, according to the promise he made to our ancestors, to Abraham and to his descendants forever," use language from Micah and 2 Samuel: "You will show faithfulness to Jacob and unswerving loyalty to Abraham, as you have sworn to our ancestors from the days of old" (Mic. 7:20); and God "shows steadfast love to his anointed, to David and his descendants forever" (2 Sam. 22:51).

So also the words of the Benedictus and Nunc Dimittis resonate with the language of ancient Israel's scriptures. As anticipated, we will not quote the passages to make the point. Readers wishing to see the echoes for themselves may look up the following verses. For the Benedictus, see Psalms 41:3; 72:18; 106:48; 111:4; 132:17; Ezekiel 29:21; 1 Samuel 2:10; Psalm 106;10; Micah 7:20; Psalm 106:45; Exodus 2:24; Psalm 105:8–9; Jeremiah 11:5; Isaiah 40:3; Malachi 3:1; Isaiah 9:2; and Psalm 107:10. And for the Nunc Dimittis, see Genesis 46:30 and Isaiah 52:10; 49:6.

We do not imagine that composing these three hymns involved a process of looking up passages in the Old Testament and then, using a cut-and-paste method, creating a pastiche. Rather, for Luke and many early Christians, the language of the Old Testament was very familiar because it was their Bible. Its phrases were their natural language of thanksgiving and praise, and the use of these phrases in these hymns underlines Luke's conviction that Jesus is the fulfillment of the Law and the Prophets.

We note one more way in which Luke uses the Old Testament. Scholars have long observed that the first two chapters of Luke were written in a style that imitates the Septuagint, the Greek translation of the Old Testament. Luke is a gifted writer, able to change literary styles at will. Deliberately imitating the style of the Septuagint said, in effect: what has happened in Jesus is the continuation and climax of the story of Israel.

Thus, in their different ways, Matthew and Luke proclaim that Jesus is the fulfillment of God's promise to Israel and of Israel's deepest yearning—for a king like the great king David, for a different kind of life and different kind of world, for light in the darkness, for the presence of God with us. A line from the late nineteenth-century hymn "O Little Town of Bethlehem" expresses this conviction with remarkable economy: "The hopes and fears of all the years are met in thee tonight."

FULFILLMENT: THE LARGER FRAMEWORK

We now set the theme of fulfillment within the larger framework of the Old Testament as a whole. Seeing this framework, rather than emphasizing individual verses as predictions, enables us to see the larger meaning of fulfillment that runs through Matthew and Luke.

Central to the Old Testament is the theme of God's promise and fulfillment. It is a major dynamic, perhaps even *the* major dynamic of the Law and the Prophets, the two parts of the Bible that had become sacred by the first century. The Law and the Prophets were the Bible for Jesus and earliest Christianity.

Promise and Fulfillment in the Law

The Law (also called the "Torah" and "Pentateuch") consists of the first five books of the Bible, Genesis through Deuteronomy. The first portion of the Jewish tradition to become sacred, to become "Bible," it combines Israel's story of its origins and the laws by which it was to live within its covenantal relationship with God. It was the foundational narrative of Israel's existence and life.

Promise and fulfillment are its overarching theme, structuring the Torah as a whole. Early in Genesis, the story of Israel's father and mother, Abraham and Sarah, begins with

God's promise to them. They are nomads without a home and childless as well, but God promises a homeland and descendants as numerous as the stars in the sky (Gen. 15:5–7; see also 12:1–2, 7). By the end of the Pentateuch, many generations later, their descendants stand on the border of the "promised land," about to become a people living in their own land. The promise to Abraham and Sarah is about to be fulfilled.

In between the promise in Genesis and its fulfillment as the Torah ends is story after story of threats to the fulfillment and God's overcoming of the threats. Abraham and Sarah are promised descendants—but they are old and barren. Nevertheless, Sarah conceives. So also Rebekah (wife of Isaac) and Rachel (wife of Jacob) are barren—but God opens their wombs.

Then the worst threat to the promise happens: the ancient Hebrews fall into slavery in Egypt and face genocide at the hands of Pharaoh, the ruler of their world. But God through Moses liberates them from Egypt and rescues them at the sea from a pursuing Egyptian army. In the wilderness, the threat to the promise is generated by Israel's lapses into faithlessness. But despite all these obstacles, God's promise is fulfilled.

The Prophets: Hope for an
Ideal King of Justice and Peace

In the Prophets, the other portion of the Jewish tradition that had reached canonical status by the time of Jesus, the promise and the problem take a different form. It is no longer about land and descendants, for the ancient Israelites had become a people living in their own land. Now the yearning and promise are for justice and peace, most often associated with the hope for an ideal king who would bring both.

This yearning was generated by the establishment of a monarchy within Israel around 1000 BCE, a few centuries after the exodus from Egypt. Before long, the monarchy had become a native domination system that oppressed and exploited most of the people. Egypt had been recreated within Israel and the Israelite king had become a new Pharaoh, to use language from the contemporary Old Testament scholar Walter Brueggemann.

The period of Israel's history covered by the Prophets concerns the rise, failure, and fall of the monarchy. With few exceptions, the kings of Israel and Judah are pronounced to have done, in the words of a frequent refrain in the books of Kings, "what was evil in the sight of the Lord."

In this setting, the prophets expressed the people's yearning for and God's promise of a transformed world. This involved them in consistent indictment of the monarchy for its injustice, violence, and idolatry. The three go together: injustice and violence are the product of loving something more than loving the "the Lord your God, who brought you out of the land of Egypt, out of the house of slavery" (Exod. 20:2). The Lord of the exodus and the lords of monarchy, of the domination system, are very different.

And so the yearning was for a different kind of king and a different kind of kingdom. The prophets yearned for and promised one who would "do justice" and "love kindness" and "walk humbly with God" (Mic. 6:8). Sometimes it took the form of hope for a son of David, a new David, the great king who ruled Israel before the monarchy became opulent and exploitative—hope for a ruler who would bring justice and peace to Israel and the world.

The hope and promise are expressed in one of the best-known passages in the Prophets, as we noted in Chapter 3. It is found in virtually identical form in Isaiah 2:2–4 and Micah 4:1–3. We first cite the portion that is essentially identical in the two prophets, and italicize the most familiar part:

> In days to come the mountain of the Lord's house [the temple in Jerusalem, built on Mt. Zion] shall be established as the highest of the mountains, and shall be raised up above the hills. Peoples shall stream to it, and many nations shall come and say, "Come, let us go up to the mountain of the Lord, to the house of the God of Jacob; that he may teach us his ways and that we may walk in his paths." For out of Zion shall go forth instruction, and the word of the Lord from Jerusalem. He shall judge between many peoples, and shall arbitrate between strong nations far away; *they shall beat their swords into plowshares, and their spears into pruning hooks; nation shall not lift up sword against nation, neither shall they learn war any more.*

Then, to this promise of a world of peace and nonviolence, Micah adds the promise of justice and a world without fear:

> But they shall all sit under their own vines and under their own fig trees, and no one shall make them afraid. (4:4)

People sitting under their own vines and fig trees is an image of everybody having their own land and therefore having a secure basis for their material existence. And it is not simply bare subsistence that is envisioned: vines and fig trees are about more than subsistence. It is an image of everybody having enough and being secure—"and no one shall make them afraid."

This is the promise that sounds through the prophets—a world of justice and peace radically different from the world of their own monarchy and the world of the nations. For them, this is the passion of the God of Israel, who brought Israel out of the land of Egypt.

By the time of Jesus, the ancient Jews had lived under one empire after another for around five hundred years. Some were worse than others, but all behaved as empires do, with their attendant oppression, injustice, and violence. The only exception to imperial rule was a century of independence under native rulers (the Maccabees, also known as the Hasmoneans) from about 164 to 63 BCE. But their rule did little to bring justice and peace. And with the introduction of Roman imperial rule in 63 BCE, the Jewish people seemed more oppressed than ever.

The hope for justice and the promise of peace had not come to pass. In this setting, the stories of the first Christmas have extraordinary power. Both Matthew and Luke proclaim: Jesus is the means through which God's promises are, and will be, fulfilled.

Conclusion: The Infancy Hymns Revisited

We conclude by returning to the three hymns in Luke as magnificent expressions of early Christian hope and fulfillment. In the words of these ancient hymns, older than the gospel of Luke, we hear not only the conviction that God's promise is being fulfilled, but also the shape, the content, of that promise and that fulfillment.

The opening lines of the Magnificat (1:46–55) are already familiar to us. Mary sings, "My soul magnifies the Lord, and my spirit rejoices in God my Savior, for he has looked with favor on the lowliness of his servant." She continues, "God's mercy is for those who fear him from generation to generation."

Then, the middle part of Mary's song recites the content of God's promise now being fulfilled. We encourage you to attempt the difficult: try to hear these familiar words for the first time.

> *God has shown strength with his arm;*
> *he has scattered the proud in the thoughts of their hearts.*
> *He has brought down the powerful from their thrones,*
> *and lifted up the lowly;*
> *he has filled the hungry with good things,*
> *and sent the rich away empty.*

Mary's song emphasizes the great reversal brought by the coming of Jesus—scattering the proud, bringing down the powerful, sending the rich away empty, lifting up the lowly, filling the hungry. Only when our ears are dulled by habituated ways of hearing do we miss the radical meaning of this language.

This is the hope expressed in Hannah's hymn, the model for Mary's:

> *The bows of the mighty are broken,*
> *but the feeble gird on strength.*
> *Those who were full have hired themselves out for bread,*
> *but those who were hungry are fat with spoil. . . .*
> *The Lord makes poor and makes rich,*
> *he brings low, he also exalts.*
> *He raises up the poor from the dust;*
> *he lifts the needy from the ash heap. (1 Sam. 2:4–5, 7–8)*

Indeed, this is the hope of the Law and the Prophets: that the world will be changed. To say the obvious, this hope is for *this*

world. It is not about life beyond death, but about the transformation of *this* world.

Then Mary's song concludes with the affirmation that this
is the fulfillment of God's promise to the ancestors of the Jewish people:

> *God has helped his servant Israel,*
>   *in remembrance of his mercy,*
> *according to the promise he made to our ancestors,*
>   *to Abraham and to his descendants forever.*

This is Luke's way of proclaiming what the coming of Jesus
means.

In the Benedictus (1:68–79), we find the same emphasis
on Jesus as the fulfillment of God's promise for the transformation of this world. Though Luke puts this hymn into
the mouth of Zechariah, the father of John the Baptizer, it is
clearly about Jesus, not John.

It begins by blessing God for what has happened: "Blessed
be the Lord God of Israel, for he has looked favorably on his
people and redeemed them." Then it speaks about Jesus as "a
mighty savior" who is the fulfillment of the prophets: "God
has raised up a mighty savior for us in the house of his servant
David, as he spoke through the mouth of his holy prophets
from of old." The result: so "that we would be saved from our
enemies and from the hand of all who hate us."

The hymn then returns to the affirmation of promise fulfilled: "Thus God has shown the mercy promised to our ancestors, and has remembered his holy covenant, the oath that
he swore to our ancestor Abraham." The result? The same as
in the earlier verse: "to grant us that we, being rescued from
the hands of our enemies, might serve him without fear, in

holiness and righteousness before him all our days." Finally, it concludes with the theme of light and peace: "By the tender mercy of our God, the dawn from on high will break upon us, to give light to those who sit in darkness and in the shadow of death, to guide our feet into the way of peace."

Like that of the Magnificat, its image of God's promise and of Jesus as a mighty savior concerns *this* world, not heaven. The early Christians who sang the Benedictus emphasized salvation from their enemies so that in *this* life they might serve God without fear all their days.

These hymns proclaim and remind us that the God of the Bible is concerned about the whole of life. There is a "spiritual" reading of these hymns and the Christmas stories as a whole that sometimes obscures this. Within this reading, their language is understood to refer primarily or only to "internal" states: the spiritually proud will be brought down, and the spiritually lowly will be lifted up; the "poor" are the spiritually poor, and they will be filled; the enemies are spiritual enemies, and so forth.

But to suppose this is to ignore the fact that this language is about how the world should be. The exclusively "spiritual" reading of this language emerged only after Christianity became the dominant religion of late Roman and then European culture. Before then, it was understood to be about *this* world and the transformation of this world.

The Magnificat and the Benedictus—and the Christmas stories and the Bible as a whole—combine what we often separate, namely, religion and politics, spirituality and a passion for this world. Are these hymns religious and spiritual? Yes. Are they also political, about a transformed world? Yes. Together, they announce, in the language of our Chapter 3, that the Great Divine Cleanup of the World has begun in Jesus.

Like Luke himself, we give the last word to the Nunc Dimittis, the third and briefest hymn. On the occasion of the presentation of the infant Jesus in the temple, Simeon, described as "righteous and devout" and "looking forward to the consolation of Israel" (2:25), sings it. "Guided by the Spirit," Simeon "took Jesus in his arms and praised God":

> Lord, now you are dismissing your servant in peace,
>   according to your word;
> for my eyes have seen your salvation,
>   which you have prepared in the presence of all peoples,
> a light for revelation to the Gentiles,
>   and for glory to your people Israel. (2:28–32)

The words of this hymn powerfully proclaim the promise and fulfillment theme. What Simeon has yearned for, what Israel has yearned for, has come to pass: in Jesus, God's salvation has come; and it is revelation to the Gentiles and glory to Israel. Simeon can die in peace.

PROPHECY FULFILLED

So, is Jesus prophecy fulfilled? Yes. And in a much richer and fuller sense than imagined by those of us who grew up with the prediction-fulfillment formula and paradigm.

Jesus is not the fulfillment of miraculously specific predictions. Rather, he is the fulfillment of the Law and the Prophets in a much more comprehensive sense. He is not their replacement, as has too often been thought by Christians, as if he superceded, and thus made irrelevant, the Law and the Prophets (and thus Judaism).

Instead, he is, according to Matthew and Luke (and the rest of the New Testament) the completion of the Law and the Prophets. He is their crystallization, their expression in an embodied life. He decisively reveals and incarnates the passion of God as disclosed in the Law and the Prophets—the promise and hope for a very different kind of world from the world of Pharaoh and Caesar, the world of domination and empire.

That Jesus is the Messiah, the Son of God, is not a fact to be proved, as if it could be the logical conclusion of a syllogism based on the argument from prophecy. Rather, to call Jesus the Messiah, the Son of God, Lord, and Savior, as the Christmas stories do, is a confession of commitment, allegiance, and loyalty. To do so means: I see in this person the anointed one of God, the decisive disclosure of God—of what can be seen of God in a human life, the fulfillment of Israel's deepest yearnings, the one who reveals God's dream for this world. This is what it means to call him Emmanuel and to affirm that Emmanuel has come.

CHAPTER NINE

JOY TO
THE WORLD

I n this our concluding chapter, we draw together three
themes. The first is joy. To say the obvious, it is the dominant tone of the celebration of Christmas. A second is
the season of Advent, the month leading up to Christmas. It is
a time of expectant anticipation and repentant preparation. A
third is the meaning of Christmas past for Christmas present
and Christmas future. What does it mean for *us now* to take
seriously what these stories meant for *them then*?

CHRISTMAS AND JOY

As we have already seen, the stories of the first Christmas are
filled with light and fulfillment—Jesus is the light in the darkness and the fulfillment of God's promise and ancient Israel's
yearning. Therefore, and not surprisingly, they are also filled

with joy. These three themes—light, fulfillment, and joy—are not separate themes, but more like threads, woven together seamlessly into a whole.

We hear the sound of joy most emphatically in Luke's story of the first Christmas. In the previous chapter, we highlighted the theme of fulfillment in Luke's three infancy hymns. Here we underline their unmistakable joy.

Their very names—the Magnificat, the Benedictus, the Nunc Dimittis—express joy. Mary sings, I magnify God because of what God is doing in me. Zechariah sings, Blessed be the Lord God of Israel who has visited and redeemed his people. Simeon sings, Now I can depart in peace for I have seen your salvation. They are songs of joy.

So also the angelic message to the shepherds (Luke 2:10, 13–14) is filled with joy: "I am bringing you good news of great joy for all the people . . ." And then:

Suddenly there was with the angel a multitude of the heavenly host, praising God and saying,

"Glory to God in the highest heaven,
and on earth peace among those whom he favors!"

As in Luke's story of Christmas then, the celebration of Christmas now is filled with joy. Consider the opening lines of familiar Christmas hymns:

Joy to the world, the Lord is come!
Let earth receive her King!

O come, all ye faithful,
joyful and triumphant.

It came upon the midnight clear,
that glorious song of old.

Hark! The herald angels sing,
Glory to the newborn King!

Angels we have heard on high,
sweetly singing o'er the plains.
. . . Gloria in excelsis Deo,

From heaven above to earth I come
to bring good news to everyone!
Glad tidings of great joy I bring.

Less familiarly, but gorgeously: "Break forth, O beauteous heavenly light, and usher in the morning."

Joy — and Conflict

The stories of the first Christmas are not only filled with joy, but also with the theme of conflict. We see this very clearly in Matthew. Though his story sounds the theme of fulfillment, its emotional tone is ominous. Driven and dominated by Herod's plot to kill Jesus, it is dark and foreboding. It speaks of the murderous resistance of the rulers of this world to the coming of the kingdom of God.

So also in Luke. Alongside and within his joyful emphasis, the theme of conflict with the powerful of this world appears (1:51–53):

God has shown strength with his arm;
    he has scattered the proud in the thoughts of their hearts.
He has brought down the powerful from their thrones,
    and lifted up the lowly;
he has filled the hungry with good things,
    and sent the rich away empty.

What is hoped for in those lines is very different from the way things are and points forward to the conflict that will be engendered by Jesus's public activity.

The ominous tone becomes even more explicit when the aged Simeon warns Mary immediately after he has sung the Nunc Dimittis:

> This child is destined for the falling and the rising of many in Israel and to be a sign that will be opposed, so that the inner thoughts of many will be revealed—and a sword will pierce your own soul also. (2:34–35)

The final phrase refers to the pain and grief that Mary herself will face because of the destiny of her son. Christmas brings joy and conflict. It did so then, and it does so now.

CHRISTMAS AND ADVENT

The stories of the first Christmas are about the present as well as the past. Marcus remembers a scene from childhood when he first learned this. He is six or seven years old, at home with his mother in the days around Christmas. As he sings the familiar Christmas hymn "Joy to the World," he sings the second line, "The Lord *has* come." His mother gently corrects him. She says, "No—the words aren't, 'The Lord *has* come.' The words are, 'The Lord *is* come.'"

At the time, he was puzzled. Surely, he thought, Christmas is about the coming of Jesus a long time ago, indeed, two thousand years ago: he *has* come. Years later, he realized that his mother and the words of the hymn are right. Christmas is about the coming in the present of the Lord who came long ago in the past. Jesus comes again each Christmas.

This is the central purpose of the season of the church year known as Advent, the four Sundays and four weeks before Christmas. Each Advent, Christians relive ancient Israel's yearning and hope, and each Christmas Christians celebrate the fulfillment of that yearning: "Joy to the world—the Lord *is* come." The purpose of Advent and Christmas is to bring the past into the present.

In the same way, this is the purpose of Lent and Holy Week, the other most sacred season of the church year. During Lent and Holy Week, the past becomes present as Christians participate in Jesus's final journey to Jerusalem, his crucifixion and resurrection. It is not just about remembering, but reliving. Indeed, this is the sacramental function of both seasons: to bring the past into the present.

The Latin root of Advent is a word that means "coming." Advent thus means "toward the coming." Advent is preparation for the coming of Jesus to the world—then, in the past; now, in the present; and, as we will see, later, in the future. Advent and Christmas bring the coming of Jesus, the birth of Jesus with all of its associations, into the present.

Advent as a reliving in the present of ancient Israel's hope and yearning is expressed in an Advent hymn more than a thousand years old. Its first verse is very familiar:

O come, O come, Emmanuel,
and ransom captive Israel,
that mourns in lonely exile here,
until the Son of God appear.

The language is evocative and powerful. We are Israel—in exile, captive, mourning, lonely, longing. Israel's longing is an epiphany of human longing.

The seventh verse explicitly universalizes the yearning: it is the desire of nations:

O come Desire of nations, bind
in one the hearts of all mankind.
Bid thou our sad divisions cease,
and be thyself our King of Peace.

At the end of each verse of this long hymn, a joyful chorus confidently proclaims its fulfillment: "Rejoice! Rejoice! Emmanuel shall come to thee, O Israel." Longing and rejoicing meet.

Past, present, and future are brought together in Advent. It is a season of expectant anticipation, of anticipatory joy. It is also a season of repentant preparation for a future that is yet to come.

Advent as Expectant Anticipation

For each Sunday in Advent, there is a set of biblical texts known as lectionary readings. More than half of the Old Testament texts are from the prophet Isaiah. The gospel texts focus on John the Baptizer and Mary the mother of Jesus. They are filled with the theme of expectant anticipation. Moreover, the anticipation, the hope, is not vague and general, but quite specific.

The texts from Isaiah for the Sundays of Advent speak of Israel's yearning and God's promise of a different kind of world:

- Isaiah 11:1–10 expresses the hope for an ideal king upon whom the Spirit of the Lord will rest. With justice, he will judge the poor and decide with equity for the meek of the earth. His reign will mean no more violence; the wolf shall live with the lamb, the leopard shall lie down with the kid, and no one shall hurt or destroy.

- Isaiah 2:1–5 expresses the hope for a world of peace: the nations "will beat their swords into plowshares and their spears into pruning hooks" and not "learn war any more."

- Isaiah 7:10–16 is about the sign of Immanuel: a child will be born whose name will be a sign that "God is with us."

- Isaiah 40.1–11 and 35:1–10 expresses the yearning to return from exile. In the wilderness, God is preparing "the way of the Lord," a path of return for those exiled in Babylon. The way shall be called "the Holy Way." For those who embark upon it, "Everlasting joy shall be upon their heads."

- Isaiah 61:1–4, 8–11 speaks about one whom the spirit of God has anointed. His task is "to bring good news to the oppressed, to bind up the brokenhearted, to proclaim liberty to the captives, and release to the prisoners."

- Isaiah 64:1–9 expresses the yearning for God: "O that you would tear open the heavens and come down." It is followed by a deep sense of contrition and the need for repentance.

So also the gospel texts for Advent sound this theme of expectant anticipation. For two Sundays, they are about John the Baptizer, the mentor and forerunner of Jesus. Like the Isaiah texts, they are filled with joyful anticipation. They speak of John as the messenger who prepares "the way of the Lord" in the wilderness and who announces the coming of one more powerful than he (Matt. 3:1–12; Mark 1:1–8; Luke 3:1–6).

In another Advent text (Matt. 11:2–11), John is in prison and soon to be executed by Herod Antipas, the ruler of his world. From prison he sends messengers to Jesus with a question: "Are you the one who is to come, or are we to wait for another?" Is Jesus the coming one, the promised one?

Jesus responds with words that echo Isaiah 35: "Go and tell John what you hear and see: the blind receive their sight, the lame walk, the lepers are cleansed, the deaf hear, the dead are raised, and the poor have good news brought to them." In Isaiah, the text is not a list of miracles, but a metaphorical description of what the time of God's salvation will be like. The gospel text affirms that Jesus is the fulfillment of the hope of Isaiah and John.

Mary is the focus of the gospel texts for the last Sunday in Advent. They include:

- Matthew 1:18–25: The story of Jesus's conception by the Holy Spirit and that he will be Emmanuel, "God with us."

- Luke 1:26–38: The annunciation to Mary by the angel Gabriel that she will bear a child conceived by the Holy Spirit, followed by Mary's obedient response.

- Luke 1:39–55: Mary's visit to Elizabeth and the Magnificat, with its joyful and subversive language about what God is doing: scattering the proud in the thoughts of their hearts, bringing down the mighty from their thrones, lifting up the lowly, filling the hungry with good things, and sending the rich empty away.

In Mary, expectation has become pregnancy. A new life, a new world, is waiting to be born.

Advent as Repentant Preparation

Advent is also a season of repentant preparation. The theme is announced on the first Sunday in Advent. The prayer for the day (called the Collect) begins: "Almighty God, give us grace to cast away the works of darkness, and to put on the armor of light, now in the time of this mortal life in which your Son Jesus Christ came to visit us in great humility." The gospel texts for this Sunday all refer to the "second coming" of Jesus in the future and urge preparedness (Matt. 24:36–44; Mark 13:24–37; Luke 21:25–36).

The theme recurs on subsequent Sundays. The prayer for the second Sunday of Advent (the Collect) begins: "Merciful God, who sent your messengers the prophets to preach repentance and prepare the way for our salvation: Give us grace to heed their warnings and forsake our sins, that we may greet with joy the coming of Jesus Christ our Redeemer." Texts about John the Baptizer highlight repentance: "Repent," "Bear fruit worthy of repentance," and "I baptize you with water for repentance" (Matt. 3:1–12; see also Mark 1:1–8; Luke 3:1–6, 7–18).

The meaning of repentance in the Bible is quite different from that in widespread postbiblical Christian understanding. Many Christians think of repentance as primarily contrition—as being sincerely sorry for our sins, confessing them,

and perhaps doing penance, but the biblical meaning emphasizes change.

Repentance as Change. To repent is to turn to God. In the
Old Testament, its meaning is shaped by the Jewish experience of exile: it means to return from exile to the place of
God's presence. The phrase "Prepare the way of the Lord,"
central to Advent, is thus about repentance: "the way of the
Lord" is the path of return from exile to God. To repent is to
turn away from the lords of this world and to turn to God, to
return to God. To repent, to return, is to follow the way that
leads out of our exile, separation, alienation, and estrangement
to reconnection.

The New Testament meaning of the word continues the
Old Testament meaning and adds an additional nuance. In
the New Testament, the root of the Greek word translated as
"repent" means "go beyond the mind that you have," to enter
into a new mind-set, a new way of seeing. To repent means to
begin seeing differently.

To repent is to change. To return to the birth stories, we may
imagine that the wise men and the shepherds were changed by
their experience. Of course, these are fictional characters. But
we are entitled to imagine the lives of fictional characters such
as, for example, the life of the prodigal son in Jesus's famous
parable. A concise phrase about the wise men in Matthew
makes their change explicit. After the guiding star led them to
Jesus and they paid him homage, they went home "by another
road." They no longer walked the same path, but followed another way.

So also we may imagine that the shepherds were changed
by their experience. They had seen the night sky filled with
the radiant luminosity of God's glory and heard angels an-
nouncing the birth of "a Savior, who is the Messiah." Though

we may imagine that the shepherds remained shepherds, they would not have been the same. In future years, they would not simply have reminisced about an "odd" experience they had one night, but they would have seen differently because of their experience. They had heard and seen that the Lord and Savior of the world, a Jewish Lord, had been born in a stable in a world ruled by an imperial lord and savior. How could they not be changed?

Repentance and Our Now. We turn to our now. What does Advent as a season of repentant preparation mean for American Christians today? The meanings of this season are both personal and political, both internal and external, both inward and outward.

On the personal level, Christmas is about light coming into the darkness of our individual lives, about our return from exile, about inner peace. Indeed, it is about the birth of Christ within us. In the thirteenth century, the Christian mystic Meister Eckhart preached about Christmas as the birth of Christ *within us* through the union of God's Spirit with our flesh. So also a line from the familiar nineteenth-century hymn "O Little Town of Bethlehem" affirms the personal meaning: "O holy child of Bethlehem . . . be born in us today."

And, like the birth stories themselves, the meaning of Advent as a season of repentant preparation is also political. For centuries, this meaning has been eclipsed by the political domestication of the gospel. It began in the fourth century when Christianity became the religion of the Roman Empire and subsequently the dominant religion of Western cultures. The imperial captivity of Advent and Christmas has a long history. But once you see the political meaning of Advent and Christmas, it seems so obvious. Not to see it seems a kind of blindness, whether habituated or willful.

In our time, American Christians need especially to see the political meanings of these stories, for we live in a time of the American empire. Not so long ago, saying that America is an imperial power was a left-wing claim. But it is no longer disputed. Many political conservatives, including those at the highest level of government, not only affirm but celebrate it—the twenty-first century is to be the century of the American empire.

We add that empire is not intrinsically about geographical expansion and territorial acquisition. As a nation, that is not our aim. Rather, empire is about the use of superior power— military, political, and economic—to shape the world as the empire sees fit. In this sense, we are the new Rome.

The responses of American Christians to the American empire cover the political spectrum. They range from enthusiastic support to conventional compliance to uncertainty to timid or assertive protest. In this setting, the anti-imperial meanings of the birth stories raise challenging questions for American Christians. Who are we in these stories?

Are we like the Magi who follow the light and refuse to comply with the ruler's plot to destroy it? Or are we like Herod, filled with fear and willing to use whatever means necessary to maintain power, even violence and slaughter? Are we among those in Herod's court who seek to thwart the coming of the true light, the true king, and God's kingdom?

Are we supporters of the dragon of Revelation, the ancient serpent who seeks to devour the newborn child and to rule the world through intimidation and fear, violence and chaos and to call it peace?

Are we among those who yearn for the coming of the kingdom of justice and peace, who seek peace through justice? Or do we, like advocates of imperial theology, seek peace through victory?

Where do we see the light of the world? Is America, the American empire, the light shining in the darkness? Jim Wallis, in his important book *God's Politics,* reports that our president on the first anniversary of the terrorist attacks of September 2001 spoke of America as "the light shining in the darkness."[1] The statement is remarkably similar to Rome's claim to be Apollo, the bringer of light. Or do we see the light of the world in Jesus, who stood against empire and indeed was executed by imperial authority?

We are aware that the above might sound like an indictment of our present president and the policies of his administration. But our point is the perennial temptation of imperial power and hubris. The peril comes from the ways of empire, not from a particular president and administration.

To return to who we are and who we might be in the stories of the first Christmas. Are we like Mary, willing to say, "Let it be with me according to your word," obedient to the role she had been given in bringing about a different kind of world?

What if we were to identify with the shepherds? They represent those of lowly status, the socially and economically marginalized. Or do we, to use words from later in the gospel, identify with "those who put on fine clothing and live in luxury in royal palaces" (Luke 7:25; Matt. 11:8)?

Perhaps few readers of this book fall into either category. But the story of the shepherds invites those of us who have some wealth and influence to become disenchanted elites, no longer mesmerized by the claims of empire to be the light and hope of the world. If we identify with the shepherds, we will dream of and seek a different kingdom, one more and more under the lordship of God as known in Jesus, revealed to them on a starry night as Messiah, Lord, and Savior.

Or are we among those who hear the story of Jesus, but aren't sure what to make of what we hear? No doubt there were many in this category who heard Jesus during his lifetime. Is this who we are?

We are meant to be changed by Advent and Christmas. This is the sacramental purpose of this season of the Christian liturgical year.

Christmas Future

In a Christmas story that has become almost as well known as the stories of the first Christmas, *A Christmas Carol,* Charles Dickens vividly portrays Scrooge's encounters with the ghosts of Christmas past, Christmas present, and Christmas future. Scrooge's experience of the three spirits changes him. And because of that change, Christmas future becomes different. Dickens got it right: Christmas has three tenses. There is a spirit of Christmas past, Christmas present, and Christmas future.

We turn now to Christmas future. Advent and Christmas are about a new world. They are thus intrinsically about eschatology. Recall what we said about this word in Chapter 3: eschatology is about the divine transformation of our earth. It is not about some mass immigration from a doomed world to a blessed heaven. Rather, it is about the end of this era of war and violence, injustice, and oppression. It is about the earth's transformation, not about its devastation. It is about a world of justice and peace.

How will this transformation of the world come about? To say the obvious, it has not yet happened, despite the passage of two thousand years. It is not yet accomplished. Does this mean that the Christmas stories are a pipe dream? That they (and the New Testament as a whole) are another example of failed eschatology, of hope become hopeless?

It depends upon how we think the new world is to come about. Two very different understandings, two different eschatologies, are found in the history of Christianity as well as in modern scholarship. We call the first one "supernatural eschatology," or "interventionist eschatology." Within this understanding, only God can bring about the new world. It can happen only through a dramatic divine intervention. All we can do is wait for it and pray for it. Many twentieth-century scholars argued that this is what Jesus and the earliest Christians expected. It has also been found in popular Christianity throughout the centuries. In our time, it is especially virulent in the violently destructive scenarios imagined by those who expect the second coming of Jesus in the near future.

We call the second one "participatory eschatology," or "collaborative eschatology." Put simply, we are to participate with God in bringing about the world promised by Christmas. Rather than waiting for God to do it, we are to collaborate with God.

There is a third option as well—namely, letting go of eschatology. This view is also found among Christians. Some do not see a connection between the gospel and a transformed earth. For them, Christianity is only about individual salvation, whether in this life or in a life beyond death. This world may be seen as a pleasant place or a dreadful place, but Christian hope is not about the transformation of this world.

We reject both the first option and the third option. We do not imagine that God will bring about a perfect world through divine intervention someday. We do not imagine a supernatural rescue of the earth. And we find the third option to be a betrayal of much of the Bible, both Old Testament and New Testament. The Christmas stories are not about a spectacular series of miraculous events that happened in the past that we are to believe in for the sake of going to heaven. Rather, they are about God's passion, God's dream, for a transformed earth.

We affirm the second option, participatory eschatology. Participatory eschatology involves a twofold affirmation: we are to do it with God, and we cannot do it without God. In St. Augustine's brilliant aphorism, God without us will not; we without God cannot. We who have seen the star and heard the angels sing are called to participate in the new birth and new world proclaimed by these stories.

The struggle between two visions of life continues. The birth stories are not a pipe dream, but a proclamation that what we see revealed in Jesus is *the* way—the way to a different kind of life and a different future. Both personal and political transformation, both the eschatology of rebirth and the eschatology of a new world, require our participation. God will not change us as individuals without our participation, and God will not change the world without our participation.

Conclusion: The Gospel in Miniature

As we have already suggested, the stories of the first Christmas contain the gospel in miniature. They do so as parabolic overtures to the two gospels in which they are found. In yet another sense, they are the gospel in miniature, for the stories of the beginning of Jesus's life are remarkably parallel to the stories of his last week—Holy Week, Good Friday, and Easter.

Just as the powers of darkness sought to quench the light in Herod's plot to kill Jesus, so they do at the end of his life. The powers that ruled his world executed him. But their success was only apparent, for his crucifixion was followed by Easter glory, radiance, and luminosity.

In the first Easter story in the gospels (Mark 16:1–8), an angel—a being of light—appears at daybreak on Easter morning and announces to the women at Jesus's tomb that they would not find Jesus among the dead, but among the living. To Paul, the risen Christ appears as a brilliant light (Acts 9, 22, 26). Paul himself speaks of the risen Christ as "the glory of the Lord" who has "shone in our hearts to give the light of the knowledge of the glory of God in the face of Jesus Christ" (2 Cor. 3:18; 4:6). Just as Jesus is the light of the world in the stories of his birth, so at Easter he is the radiant glory of God.

Archbishop Oscar Romero, a twentieth-century Christian martyr killed by the powers that ruled El Salvador, once said that we are called to be Easter Christians in a Good Friday world, in a world still ruled by Herod and Caesar. So also we are called to be Christmas Christians in a world that still descends into darkness. But Good Friday and the descent of darkness do not have the final word—unless we let them.

Jesus is already the light in the darkness for those who follow him. Conceived by the Spirit and christened as Son of God by the community that grew up around him, he is, for Christians, Emmanuel: "God with us."

We give the last word to one of the carols of Christmas we mentioned earlier, one of the songs we sing in the midst of winter darkness. It combines the themes of Advent and

Christmas in a remarkable way: joy to the world, the political images of Jesus as Lord and king, the personal image of every heart preparing room for him, and the rejoicing of heaven and nature, the whole of creation:

> *Joy to the world, the Lord is come.*
> *Let earth receive her King!*
> *Let every heart prepare him room,*
> *And heaven and nature sing,*
> *And heaven and nature sing,*
> *And heaven, and heaven, and nature sing.*

Joy to the world—for God so loves the world.

THE GENEALOGIES OF JESUS IN MATTHEW AND LUKE

STRUCTURE OF MATTHEW 1:1–17

(Names common to Matthew and Luke are italicized)

1. (1) *Abraham* → *Isaac*	1. *David* → Solomon	1. Jechoniah → *Salathiel*
2. (2) *Isaac* → *Jacob*	2. (1) Solomon → Rehoboam	2. (1) *Salathiel* → *Zerubbabel*
3. (3) *Jacob* → *Judah*	3. (2) Rehoboam → Abijah	3. (2) *Zerubbabel* → Abiud
4. (4) *Judah* → *Perez*	4. (3) Abijah → Asaph	4. (3) Abiud → Eliakim
5. (5) *Perez* → *Hezron*	5. (4) Asaph → Jehoshaphat	5. (4) Eliakim → Azor
6. (6) *Hezron* → Aram	6. (5) Jehoshaphat → Joram	6. (5) Azor → Zadok
7. (7) Aram → *Aminadab*	7. (6) Joram → Uzziah	7. (6) Zadok → Achim
8. (8) *Aminadab* → Nahshon	8. (7) Uzziah → Jotham	8. (7) Achim → Eliud
9. (9) *Nahshon* → *Salmon*	9. (8) Jotham → Ahaz	9. (8) Eliud → Eleazar

10. (10) *Salmon* →   10. (9) Ahaz →   10. (9) Eleazar →
      Boaz   Hezekiah   Matthan

11. (11) *Boaz* →   11. (10) Hezekiah →   11. (10) Matthan →
      Obed   Manasseh   Jacob

12. (12) *Obed* →   12. (11) Manasseh →   12. (11) Jacob →
      Jesse   Amos   (12) *Joseph*

13. (13) *Jesse* →   13. (12) Amos →   13. Mary →
      (14) *David*   Josiah   (13) Jesus

                          14. (13) Josiah →
                               (14) Jechoniah

TEXT OF MATTHEW 1:1–17

An account of the genealogy of Jesus the Messiah, the son of David, the son of Abraham.

Abraham was the father of Isaac, and Isaac the father of Jacob, and Jacob the father of Judah and his brothers, and Judah the father of Perez and Zerah by Tamar, and Perez the father of Hezron, and Hezron the father of Aram, and Aram the father of Aminadab, and Aminadab the father of Nahshon, and Nahshon the father of Salmon, and Salmon the father of Boaz by Rahab, and Boaz the father of Obed by Ruth, and Obed the father of Jesse, and Jesse the father of King David.

And David was the father of Solomon by the wife of Uriah, Solomon the father of Rehoboam, and Rehoboam the father of Abijah, and Abijah the father of Asaph, and Asaph the father of Jehoshaphat, and Jehoshaphat the father of Joram, and Joram the father of Uzziah, and

Uzziah the father of Jotham, and Jotham the father of Ahaz, and Ahaz the father of Hezekiah, and Hezekiah the father of Manasseh, and Manasseh the father of Amos, and Amos the father of Josiah, and Josiah the father of Jechoniah and his brothers, at the time of the deportation to Babylon.

And after the deportation to Babylon: Jechoniah was the father of Salathiel, and Salathiel the father of Zerubbabel, and Zerubbabel the father of Abiud, and Abiud the father of Eliakim, and Eliakim the father of Azor, and Azor the father of Zadok, and Zadok the father of Achim, and Achim the father of Eliud, and Eliud the father of Eleazar, and Eleazar the father of Matthan, and Matthan the father of Jacob, and Jacob the father of Joseph the husband of Mary, of whom Jesus was born, who is called the Messiah.

So all the generations from Abraham to David are fourteen generations; and from David to the deportation to Babylon, fourteen generations; and from the deportation to Babylon to the Messiah, fourteen generations.

STRUCTURE OF LUKE 3:23–38

(Names common to Matthew and Luke are italicized)

(1) GOD → Adam	(8) Enoch → Methuselah
(2) Adam → Seth	(9) Methuselah → Lamech
(3) Seth → Enos	(10) Lamech → Noah
(4) Enos → Cainan	(11) Noah → Shem
(5) Cainan → Mahalaleel	(12) Shem → Arphaxad
(6) Mahalaleel → Jared	(13) Arphaxad → Cainan
(7) Jared → Enoch	(14) Cainan → Shelah

(15) Shelah → Eber
(16) Eber → Pelag
(17) Pelag → Reu
(18) Reu → Serug
(19) Serug → Nahor
(20) Nahor → Terah
(21) Terah → *Abraham*

(22) *Abraham → Isaac*
(23) *Isaac → Jacob*
(24) *Jacob → Judah*
(25) *Judah → Perez*
(26) *Perez → Hezron*
(27) *Hezron* → Arni
(28) Arni → Admin

(29) Admin → *Amminadab*
(30) *Amminadab → Nahshon*
(31) *Nahshon → Sala*
(32) *Sala → Boaz*
(33) *Boaz → Obed*
(34) *Obed → Jesse*
(35) *Jesse → David*

(36) *David* → Nathan
(37) Nathan → Mattatha
(38) Mattatha → Menna
(39) Menna → Melea
(40) Melea → Eliakim
(41) Eliakim → Jonam
(42) Jonam → Joseph

(43) Joseph → Judah
(44) Judah → Simeon
(45) Simeon → Levi
(46) Levi → Matthat

(47) Matthat → Jorim
(48) Jorim → Eliezer
(49) Eliezer → Joshua

(50) Joshua → Er
(51) Er → Elmadam
(52) Elmadam → Cosam
(53) Cosam → Addi
(54) Addi → Melchi
(55) Melchi → Neri
(56) Neri → *Shealtiel*

(57) *Shealtiel → Zerubbabel*
(58) *Zerubbabel* → Rhesa
(59) Rhesa → Joanan
(60) Joanan → Joda
(61) Joda → Josech
(62) Josech → Semein
(63) Semein → Mattathias

(64) Mattathias → Maath
(65) Maath → Naggai
(66) Naggai → Esli
(67) Esli → Nahum
(68) Nahum → Amos
(69) Amos → Mattathias
(70) Mattathias → Joseph

(71) Joseph → Jannai
(72) Jannai → Melchi
(73) Melchi → Levi
(74) Levi → Matthat
(75) Matthat → Heli
(76) Heli → *Joseph*
(77) *Joseph* [→] Jesus

TEXT OF LUKE 3:23–38

Jesus was ... the son (as was thought) of Joseph son of Heli, son of Matthat, son of Levi, son of Melchi, son of Jannai, son of Joseph, son of Mattathias, son of Amos, son of Nahum, son of Esli, son of Naggai, son of Maath, son of Mattathias, son of Semein, son of Josech, son of Joda, son of Joanan, son of Rhesa, son of Zerubbabel, son of Shealtiel, son of Neri, son of Melchi, son of Addi, son of Cosam, son of Elmadam, son of Er, son of Joshua, son of Eliezer, son of Jorim, son of Matthat, son of Levi, son of Simeon, son of Judah, son of Joseph, son of Jonam, son of Eliakim, son of Melea, son of Menna, son of Mattatha, son of Nathan, son of David, son of Jesse, son of Obed, son of Boaz, son of Sala, son of Nahshon, son of Amminadab, son of Admin, son of Arni, son of Hezron, son of Perez, son of Judah, son of Jacob, son of Isaac, son of Abraham, son of Terah, son of Nahor, son of Serug, son of Reu, son of Peleg, son of Eber, son of Shelah, son of Cainan, son of Arphaxad, son of Shem, son of Noah, son of Lamech, son of Methuselah, son of Enoch, son of Jared, son of Mahalaleel, son of Cainan, son of Enos, son of Seth, son of Adam, son of God.

COMMENTS

It is not clear how far to push the parabolic mathematics used certainly by Matthew and possibly by Luke.

Matthew certainly emphasizes 3 × 14 generations. But it is not clear that we should extend that to 6 × 7 generations, so that he intends to think of Jesus's community or the kingdom of God as the seventh generation.

Luke may have structured his genealogy in 11 × 7 generations but, since he never mentions that number or speaks of "generations," it is not certain. Furthermore, even if it were, what would that 11 indicate?

In the structure of the two genealogies of Matthew and Luke, we have italicized the names they have exactly in common. Also, to facilitate that comparison, we give both genealogies in the same father-to-son sequence by reversing the son-to-father order in Luke.

LUKE'S PARALLELISM BETWEEN JESUS AND JOHN THE BAPTIZER

The following details are based, with appreciation and gratitude, on Joseph Fitzmyer's magisterial two-volume commentary *The Gospel According to Luke* (Garden City, NY: Doubleday, 1981–85, pp. 314–15).

Annunciations of the Two Births

Zechariah and Elizabeth (1:5–7)	Mary and Joseph (1:27)
Location in temple (1:8–10)	Location in Nazareth (1:26)
Angel Gabriel appears to Zechariah (1:11, 19)	Angel Gabriel appears to Mary (1:26, 28)
Zechariah is "terrified" (1:12)	Mary is "perplexed" (1:29)
"Do not be afraid, Zechariah" (1:13a)	"Do not be afraid, Mary" (1:30a)
"Elizabeth will bear you a son" (1:13b)	"You will . . . bear a son" (1:31b)
"You will name him John" (1:13c)	"You will name him Jesus" (1:31c)
"He will be great" (1:15a)	"He will be great" (1:32a)
Child's destiny described (1:15b–17)	Child's destiny described (1:32b–33)
"How will I know that this is so?" (1:18a)	"How can this be?" (1:34a)

Problem: because of sterility (1:18b)

Problem: because of virginity (1:34b)

Sign: "You will become mute" (1:20)

Sign: Aged, barren Elizabeth pregnant (1:36)

Zechariah departs (1:23)

Gabriel departs (1:38)

Presentations of the Two Infants

"The time came for Elizabeth to give birth, and she bore a son" (1:57)

Mary "gave birth to her firstborn son" (2:7)

"On the eighth day they came to circumcise the child" (1:59)

"After eight days had passed, it was time to circumcise the child" (2:21a)

"He is to be called John" (1:60)

"He was called Jesus" (2:21b)

Zechariah's prophecy by "Holy Spirit" (1:67)

Simeon's prophecy by "Holy Spirit" (2:25, 27)

Zechariah's Benedictus hymn (1:68–79)

Simeon's Nunc Dimittis hymn (2:29–32)

Reaction of hearers (1:65–66)

Reaction of hearers (2:33)

"The child grew and became strong" (1:80)

"The child grew and became strong" (2:40)

JESUS'S COMING-OF-AGE IN LUKE

When Augustus was assuming the gown of manhood,
his senatorial tunic was ripped apart on both sides and
fell at his feet, which some interpreted as a sure sign that the
[senatorial] order of which the tunic was the badge,
would one day be brought to his feet.

—Suetonius, *Lives of the Caesars:*
The Deified Augustus (94.10)

Ancient texts often recorded a genealogy, a conception, a birth, or a coming-of-age story as a parabolic overture to the later lives of extraordinary, transcendent, or divine human beings. The Christmas stories of both Matthew and Luke use those first three events in that way, but only Luke adds the fourth, a coming-of-age story about Jesus, in 2:41–52:

Now every year his parents went to Jerusalem for the festival of the Passover. And when he was twelve years old, they went up as usual for the festival. When the festival was ended and they started to return, the boy Jesus stayed behind in Jerusalem, but his parents did not know it. Assuming that he was in the group of travelers, they went a day's journey. Then they started to look for him among their relatives and friends. When they did not find him, they returned to Jerusalem to search for him. After three days they found him in the temple, sitting among the teachers, listening to them and asking them questions. And all who heard him were amazed at his understanding and his answers. When his parents saw him they were astonished; and his mother said to him, "Child, why have you treated us like this? Look, your father and I have been searching for you in great anxiety." He said to them, "Why were you searching for me? Did you not know that I must be in my Father's house?" But they did not understand what he said to them. Then he went down with them and came to Nazareth, and was obedient to them. His mother treasured all these things in her heart.

And Jesus increased in wisdom and in years, and in divine and human favor.

That story emphasizes two aspects of Jesus as he makes the transition from late childhood to young adulthood. The first, and minor one, is his extraordinary wisdom. That is displayed in a duel of questions and answers, with each side taking the measure of the other's knowledge. That is why the key comment is: "All who heard him were amazed at his understanding (*synesis*) and his answers" (2:47). So far, however, that fits in its Jewish context.

You will recall Josephus's autobiographical *Life* in Chapter 4. Here is how he described his own coming-of-age story:

I made great progress in my education, gaining a reputation for an excellent memory and understanding (*synesis*). While still a mere boy, about fourteen years of age, I
won universal applause for my love of letters; inasmuch
that the chief priests and the leading men of the city used
constantly to come to me for precise information on some
particular in our ordinances. (8–9)

But an emphasis on Jesus's wisdom is not the main point
of Luke's story. He could have done that by having the family
take Jesus into the temple and the interchange with the teachers take place in their presence.

The second and major point needed that conversation between Jesus and his parents. The story of their search for him
allowed Jesus to say: "Why were you searching for me? Did
you not know that I must be in my Father's house?" (2:49). Why
is that so important?

At the annunciation, Gabriel told Mary that her child
would be called "the Son of the Most High" and "the Son
of God" (1:32, 35). At Jesus's baptism, God announced from
heaven, "You are my Son, the Beloved; with you I am well
pleased" (3:22). In the temple, in between those two heavenly
proclamations of Jesus's sonship, Luke places this statement
by Jesus himself. Luke's Jesus is fully conscious of his divine
status and asserts to his parents—but publicly—that he is the
Son of God and this is his Father's house.

Luke had concluded the presentation of Jesus in the temple
with this: "The child grew and became strong, filled with wisdom; and the favor of God was upon him" (2:40). And he now
concludes the finding of Jesus in the temple with this: "Jesus
increased in wisdom and in years, and in divine and human
favor" (2:52).

ACKNOWLEDGMENTS

This book, like most books, has a multitude of ancestors and a number of midwives. Its ancestors include a host of predecessors and contemporaries in the world of scholarship. Because we have written this book with the barest minimum of footnotes, they remain largely unacknowledged by name. There are two reasons. One is a convention of contemporary publishing; publishers prefer that a book written for a general reading audience not be encumbered with what can be the intimidating apparatus of academic writing. The second reason is about us. Together, we have been involved in the scholarly study of Jesus for over ninety years. Over that time, there has been an enormous accumulation of indebtedness to our academic forebears, and we find it virtually impossible to identify our specific academic debts.

However, for readers who want to know more about the scholarly study of the birth stories, we especially recommend these recent books. All happen to be by Roman Catholic scholars. Joseph A. Fitzmyer's two-volume *The Gospel According to Luke* (Garden City, NY: Doubleday, 1981–85) covers the infancy narrative on pages 303–448. John P. Meier, in the first volume of his ongoing and multivolume *A Marginal Jew* (New York: Doubleday, 1991), devotes pages 203–433 to "Roots of the Person," with chapters about Jesus's birth. Raymond E. Brown's *The Birth of the Messiah* (New York: Doubleday, 1993) is the most thorough; that second edition is 752 pages long. Finally, Robert J. Miller's *Born Divine: The Births of Jesus and Other Sons of God* (Santa Rosa, CA: Polebridge, 2003) is a 337-page treatment.

Our book's midwives include especially several members of the staff of HarperOne, our publisher. They include Mickey Maudlin, Mark Tauber, Claudia Boutote, Terri Leonard, Jan Weed, Emily Grandstaff, Lisa Zuniga, and Ann Moru.

To all of them, we are grateful.

NOTES

Chapter 2: Parables as Overtures

1. Barbara Tuchman, *The Guns of August* (New York: Macmillan, 1962), p. 522.

2. Tuchman, *Guns of August,* p. 523.

3. Stephen E. Ambrose, *Undaunted Courage: Meriwether Lewis, Thomas Jefferson, and the Opening of the American West* (New York: Simon & Schuster, 1996), p. 19.

Chapter 4: Genealogy as Destiny

1. Raymond E. Brown, *The Birth of the Messiah: A Commentary on the Infancy Narratives in the Gospels of Matthew and Luke* (New York: Doubleday, 1993), p. 74.

Chapter 6: In David's City of Bethlehem

1. John J. Collins, *The Scepter and the Star: The Messiahs of the Dead Sea Scrolls and Other Ancient Literature* (New York: Doubleday, 1995), pp. 68, 209.

2. Collins, *Scepter and the Star,* pp. 13, 204.

3. Adolf Gustav Deissmann, *Light from the Ancient East: The New Testament Illustrated by Recently Discovered Texts of the Graeco-Roman World,* trans. Lionel R. M. Strachan, Limited Editions Library (Grand Rapids, MI: Baker, 1965), p. 349.

Chapter 9: Joy to the World

1. Jim Wallis, *God's Politics: A New Vision for Faith and Politics in America* (San Francisco: HarperSanFrancisco, 2005), p. 142.